A History
of
Harlan County

A History
of
Harlan County

Mabel Green Condon

COMMONWEALTH BOOK COMPANY
St. Martin, Ohio

Copyright © 1962 by Mabel Green Condon
Copyright © 2024 by Commonwealth Book Company, Inc.

All rights reserved. No part of this book may be reproduced in any form or by any means without the prior written consent of the publisher, excepting brief quotes used in reviews. Printed in the United States of America.

ISBN: 978-1-948986-79-3

FRONT COVER IMAGE: POSTCARD VIEW OF HARLAN, KY, CIRCA 1930

Over a period of thirty-five years I have been collecting bits of Harlan County history by personal interview and correspondence from some two hundred persons. It is really an oral history, having been handed down by word of mouth from grandparents to grandchildren.

Each person was sincere in telling the tradition and recounted it to the best of his or her recollection.

If this version is different from the one you have heard, you will see that basically the accounts are true and many of these traditions have been verified by Bible, Cemetery and Court records.

Sincerely,

MABEL GREEN CONDON

CONTENTS

CHAPTER PAGE

I. Origin of Harlan County 7
II. Mount Pleasant, the County Seat 15
III. Early Scouts 29
IV. Homes 36
V. Furniture, etc. 42
VI. Topography 48
VII. Trees 56
VIII. Animals 66
IX. People, Ancestry, Negroes, etc. 74
X. Religion 84
XI. Schools 93
XII. Customs 100
XIII. Arts, Music, Poetry 110
XIV. Indians 114
XV. Milling and Trades 121
XVI. Business and Banking 128
XVII. Travel and Communications 138
XVIII. Medicine 148
XIX. Recipes, Receipts 162
XX. Superstitious Sayings 170
XXI. Pastimes 179
XXII. Politics, Laws, Court Procedures 185
XXIII. Wars 196

CHAPTER I

ORIGIN OF HARLAN COUNTY

THE town which is now Harlan was in an unmapped land when Virginia claimed it under her 1609 Charter. The Cherokee Nation, the Big Six Iroquois tribes, claimed it as their hunting ground in 1763. Only a few Indians actually lived here permanently; rather, they used it for their hunting ground.

It is told that Dr. Thomas Walker (1715-1794), a scout for the Loyal Land Company, came through Cumberland Gap in 1750 and got as far as what is now Barbourville. He kept a record of his trip and named the mountain, gap and river after the Duke of Cumberland. In 1752 a man named Finley came down the Ohio from the north as far as the Falls (now Louisville), and when he returned he told such glowing tales about the land that Daniel Boone heard of it. By the time Boone was able to make the trip it was about 1765 and shortly after numerous travelers followed the trail he blazed.

In 1775 Dick Henderson with other promoters met with more than a thousand Cherokees in a pow wow on the Wautauga River, and there they agreed to buy all the land from the Indians south of the Ohio River between the Cumberland and Kentucky rivers. This land was named Transylvania and soon after Boone founded Boonesborough, then in the county of Fincastle, Virginia.

Kentucky County was a county of Virginia in 1780 and was divided into three counties: Fayette, Jefferson and Lincoln; the latter county of Lincoln took in what is now Harlan.

For several years this land had been called Transylvania and many of the early settlers bought and paid for their land. Virginia protested the Henderson land deal and some sort of settlement was made with Henderson whereby he received some land for compensation and the men who had bought their land from him were able to hold their land title as valid so apparently everyone was satisfied.

Again Kentucky County was called Kentucky with the boundary of the present state almost the same as the original Kentucky County. It was commonly called Caintuck, Kaintuck and Kaintucky which to the Indians meant Dark and Bloody Ground.

Virginia was so busy with Eastern affairs that she could not pay enough attention to the Western frontier that was Kentucky and the early settlers became "afeared" that they could not live in the untamed country.

A big battle was fought at Blue Lick Springs in 1782 where sixty Kentuckians lost their lives. Among them were Capt. Wm. McBride, Daniel Boone's son and a renowned soldier named Major Silas Harlan. This battle is commemorated at Blue Lick Battlefield State Park and has been referred to as the last battle of the Revolution.

Harlan, who was about thirty years old and not married, left his possessions to a brother. Legend has it that he left a Bible, sword, belt pistol, musket, powder pouch and leather weskit.

The Kentuckians were becoming dissatisfied because of Virginia's lack of attention, and by 1792 when Henry Lee was governor Kentucky became the fourteenth state, although it is still a commonwealth. Danville was the first capital and remained so for several years. Isaac Shelby was the first governor of Kentucky and is buried a few miles from Danville.

A census was taken in 1790 and the only towns mentioned were

                Lexington   834
                Washington 462 on Ohio River
                Bardstown 216
                Louisville   350
                Danville   150

The counties listed were
                Bourbon population 7,830
                Fayette 18,410

ORIGIN OF HARLAN COUNTY

Jefferson 4,765
Lincoln 6,548
Madison 5,772
Mason (Washington is Co.
  seat) 2,729

Our first county seat was near Crab Orchard Springs, and the records can be found in the county seat of Lincoln County up until the year 1799 when Knox County was formed and included our section, with Barbourville the county seat. From 1799 to 1819 Harlan County records can be found at Barbourville and from 1819 the records are in our Harlan County Courthouse. Harlan County was taken from Knox and Floyd counties and then in 1842 Letcher County was taken off Perry and Harlan; in 1867 Bell was formed from Harlan and Knox; and in 1878 Leslie was formed out of Clay, Perry and Harlan so that the boundaries of Harlan today are about fifteen to twenty miles wide and about fifty miles long.

Bell County went by the name of Josh Bell County for many years.

During the Civil War the Harlan County Courthouse was burned and I shall tell you about it in another chapter. However, some of the records were saved because the clerk's office kept some of the books in an old log building which had been part of the original Harlan County Courthouse property. These books are now in our courthouse and some of the records have been type-copied. However, the old flowing handwriting is interesting and hard to read because some of the "esses" are made like "f."

Kentucky became a Commonwealth State in 1792. There was no distinct party and the state operated under joint control until 1825. The first governor was Isaac Shelby, a Revolutionary hero. Then followed James Garrard, Christopher Greenup, Charles Scott, Isaac Shelby. George Madison died in office and Gabriel Slaughter became acting governor. Then came John Adair, Joseph Desha and Thomas Metcalfe who was a National. John Breathitt was a Democrat and died in office; then James Moorehead became acting governor. James Clark belonged to the Whig-Republican Party and died in office; Charles Wickliffe became acting governor. Then followed Robert Letcher, William Owsley, John J. Crittenden who resigned to become Attorney General; John Helm, a Democrat, served out his unexpired term. Then came Lazarus Powell, Charles Moorehead, American Party, then Beriah McGoffin, a Democrat, James Robinson, Thomas Bremlett. John Helm died in office and John Stevenson became governor. He resigned to become U. S. Senator and Preston Leslie served out the term. Then came James B. McCreary, Luke Blackburn was a Democrat, J. Proctor Knott, Simon B. Buckner, and John Y. Brown—all Democrats. There came a money panic about 1896 and afterward William Bradley, a Republican, was elected. Then came William Taylor, Republican, who was opposed by William Goebel who contested the election which had been certified to William Taylor. Goebel was shot coming down the Capitol steps, but was sworn in on his deathbed. William Taylor fled the state and J. C. W. Beckham, a Democrat, served out the term. Then came Governor Alford, Augustus Wilson, James McCreary, Ed O'Rear, A. Owsley Stanley, Ed Morrow, Republican, Flem D. Sampson, Republican, and then Governor Fields, Ruby Lafoon, A. B. "Happy" Chandler, Keen Johnson, Earl C. Clements, Lawrence Weatherbey, A. B. Chandler, and Bert Combs, a Democrat who is still in office as of 1962.

You will notice that many of our Kentucky counties are named for governors. There are many names in our county which were given to babies during the administration of various governors, who left namesakes behind them.

The only President who ever visited Harlan County was Franklin Delano Roosevelt. During his Uncle Ted's administration he came to Harlan County along with his Uncle Warren Delano whose rich family had bought up boundaries with a landholding company. In Eleanor Roosevelt's book *This Is My Story* published by Harper, 1937, pages 153-54, her husband wrote her:

ORIGIN OF HARLAN COUNTY

Pennington Gap, Va., Friday Evening, June 12, '08
Pennington Gap, Va., Monday Morning, June 15

This letter head is erroneous as to our location as we have come many miles into the mountains, staying at Mr. Henry Smith's house about three miles from Harlan. We got up Sat. Morning at Pennington at 6 A.M. took the train 18 miles down the valley to Hagan and found horses waiting at the station. . . . We had some chocolate and spring water for lunch, at 2 o'clock and then started over Black Mountain on a so-called wagon road—positively the worst road I have ever seen or imagined and one which was not really easy to traverse on horseback. We dropped down

Stone Mountain Road leading to Virginia

into the valley along Catron's Creek and came to this house about 6:30 having done 22 or 23 miles in all, most of it the roughest trail and worst road in a county famous throughout the land for bad trails and worse roads.

The house belongs to Mr. Henry Smith, about the most prosperous farmer of the county, and his bottomlands along the valley are splendid. I must close this epistle hurriedly as the mail is going. Will add this PM.

A HISTORY OF HARLAN COUNTY

Harlan PM Monday.
I had to Close. . . . On Sunday we breakfasted very late at Mr. Smith's, 7 o'clock, and sat around for an hour discussing legal and political affairs, and soon rode into Harlan, about 3½ miles, which means about 7 miles anywhere else because of the horrible conditions of the roads here. . . .

This afternoon we are just back from a ride of five or six miles up Martin's Fork, the most beautiful country we have seen yet. The sides of the valley going up 2,000 feet, heavily wooded with great poplars, chestnuts and a dozen or two other deciduous trees and every mile or so a fertile bottom with fine crops and a stream of splendid water. I will add to this in the morning. Tuesday, Can't add just off for an all-day ride up Clover Fork.

Franklin Delano Roosevelt was a young man at this time, having graduated from Harvard, and his job in Harlan County was to abstract titles and surveys. He was very agile and would get on and off his horse leap-frog fashion. As we think of President Franklin Delano Roosevelt, it does not bring up memories of a young collegiate fellow who wore a turtle-neck sweater with a large "H" on it while he was working in Harlan County, but that is the way the old-timers described him. He and his Uncle Warren Delano were both friendly and would drop into stores and visit with the loafers and exchange greetings and spin yarns with the best of them. My father had a frame country-style store on the courthouse square and on cool mornings the men sat around a pot-bellied stove and spit on the hot stove. The sizzling noise this made on the hot stove fascinated young F.D.R. and soon he was sizzling louder than the old-timers.

The Kentenia Corporation, a landholding company with acreages in Kentucky, Tennessee and Virginia, was organized in 1907 with headquarters for this area in Harlan County. This company did more to develop this end of the state than anything that had come to Harlan. They were instrumental in getting the Louisville and Nashville Railroad to build a branch line into the county.

Local men who took stock in the corporation were: Lee

Kentenia Corporation Anniversary Dinner 1908—*Left to right:* Lawyer Chockley, Va., Robert Lee Ball, Charles Henry Davis, Mass., Dick Fish, Mass., Marion D. Smith, Atty. Anderson, Va., Will W. Noe, Hamp H. Howard, Arthur B. Cornett, Billie T. Rice, Lawrence K. Rice, George L. Taylor, Va., J. F. Bullett, Va., Dan Farmer (with beard), John B. Lewis, Lem Pope, W. H. Henry Smith, Will Ward Duffield, John White Farmer, Tony Helmboldt, Mass., George W. Green.

Ball, Arthur Cornett, Dan Farmer, George W. Green, Hamp H. Howard, W. W. Duffield, John White Farmer, John B. Lewis, W. W. Lewis, Lem Pope, Billie T. Rice, Marion Smith, W. H. H. (Henry) Smith, Lawrence K. Rice and Will W. Noe.

Stockholders from other states were: Warren Delano, uncle of Franklin D. Roosevelt, Charles Henry Davis of South Yarmouth, Massachussetts, president, J. F. Bullitt, Big Stone Gap, Va., vice-president, George L. Taylor, Big Stone Gap, Va., secretary, Will Ward Duffield, treasurer.

The main offices for this corporation were at Big Stone Gap, Va.

First Anniversary Dinner given by Kentenia Corporation at George W. Green's, Harlan, Kentucky, March 10, 1908.

MENU

First Course

*Shaddocks with Claret Wine

Second Course

Oyster Soup—Crackers—Olives

Third Course

Roast Turkey with Cranberry Sauce
Potatoes—String Beans—Asparagus
Corn Bread—Biscuit
Celery—Mixed Pickles
Port Wine

Fourth Course

Baked Ham with Currant Jelly
French Peas—Saratoga Chips—Chicken Salad
Sauterne

Fifth Course

Scalloped Oysters—Lettuce and Tomato Salad
Salted Almonds—Cheese—Toasted Crackers

Sixth Course

Ice Cream—Cakes—Candies
Fruit—Coffee—Ginger Ale
Curaqua
Cigars and Cigarettes

Place cards were elaborate with raised holly leaf design all the way around the edges and a green and red holly spray in one corner.

* (Shaddocks—now called grapefruit)

CHAPTER II

MOUNT PLEASANT, THE COUNTY SEAT

WHEN Harlan became a county in 1819, it was named in honor of Major Silas Harlan who fell at the Battle of Blue Lick. At that time there were only a few settlers in the county which included Yellow Creek to Cumberland Gap, Cumberland Ford which is now Pineville, and Pine Mountain to the north and east with the boundary touching Virginia on the east and south. The county of Harlan purchased twelve acres of land and built a log courthouse and two-story jail with apartment for the jailer's family.

A path led through the fields to a cow ford across Clover Fork at Mount Pleasant and a road was surveyed going north and south which is practically the same line that Main Street now runs.

George Brittain, a lieutenant colonel in the War of 1812, served in the House at Frankfort and was instrumental in getting Harlan made into a county. He became the first county court clerk.

The notes which I have on the Harlan courthouse do not entirely agree with other writers who have described the first courthouse. My own grandfather who was born in 1828 said his father brought him to the county seat once when he was a little boy and he said the courthouse was on the river bank. Both Mr. Albert Ball and Mr. Robert L. Ball told me that their grandfather had told them that there was a natural mound on the river bank with a grove of walnut trees on it which was selected for the site of this first courthouse. The construction was of logs and probably used some of the walnut trees, they thought. It had a dirt floor, one door and maybe two windows. They thought there was no way to heat it. One old man told me that when they had to ride a long distance in the cold to come to the courthouse, they brought heated sandstones for foot warmers. There were handmade log benches and rough tables made of split logs.

These men definitely described the site of the courthouse as being near the back end of what is known as the Harlan Theatre and at the east side of Black Motor Company. In 1929 when I interviewed several people who were old then, there was no one for sure who knew whether the log courthouse had any way to heat it.

However, there were several people who remembered the two-story log jail because it was not torn down when the log courthouse was torn down. At that time there was a dungeon dug out of the ground under the jail that was covered with lattice work of iron. This building stood about where Bower's store is at the corner of Clover and Main. There was another log building called the office and it is supposed that it was the clerk's office. It stood about where the corner of Main and Clover is now and the building there at present was built by William A. Brock. This office was later used for a schoolhouse and Felix G. Lewis, born 1852, recalled that he went to school in that office.

About 1838 the county commissioners decided that a new courthouse was needed so it was built of brick baked here of Harlan clay. The old brickyard kiln stood about where the west side of the Methodist Church is at present.

The new brick courthouse was built on a different site from the old log courthouse because they wanted to use the original building while the new one was under construction. The new one was placed about where the west end of the Christian Church now stands with the front facing on Main Street about where Scott's store stands. There was a side entrance which came out about where the Dr. Clark Bailey building is now located and an entrance on Clover Street. While grading the land for the new building, many Indian relics were found. What impressed the "sidewalk bosses" was the skulls and bones which were thought to be Indians because it was known that these mounds were called Indian Burying Grounds. Some of the bones were said to be in a sitting position. Beads, trinkets and iron pots were found. During the Civil War the courthouse was burned by Rebels in retaliation for the burning of a courthouse in Lee County,

MOUNT PLEASANT, THE COUNTY SEAT

Va., which was blamed on soldiers who fled into Harlan County.

After this courthouse burned, Harlan County needed a courthouse. Bids were advertised for the construction of a frame building with a two-story frame jailhouse with apartment for the jailer. The site of the building was to be where the brick one was. A separate clerk's office was designed to keep the books in so that in case of fire, it would be easier to rescue the records, some of which had been saved because some of the books were in the clerk's old log house.

Ben A. Rice, a Tazewell, Tenn., resident, who was working in Pineville at that time, was the successful bidder. He built a grist mill with saw mill attachment and all the lumber was sawed at this mill which was across the road from the site of the courthouse. He built his own home near this mill and it was the first frame building in town. It had a store-bought mantel which was the first in the county. The house was torn down in 1961 for a parking lot.

The new courthouse was built in a semicircle, rotunda style inside with seats graduating upward to a balcony. Upstairs were a jury room and a room for the Masonic Hall. This hall was also used for a schoolroom where many of the old-timers learned their three R's. My own mother went to school there when John A. Ward was a teacher. The Wards had the reputation of being fine scribes. Rella Howard Skidmore said she went to school there when Joe Ball was the schoolmaster.

This frame courthouse was used for many purposes other than for holding court long after the next courthouse was built in 1888. Meetings, preachings, schools, revivals, Sunday schools and funerals were held there. It was probably bought or leased by the Masonic Order, for it stood there many years until it burned.

By 1888 the frame courthouse was outgrown and it was decided to build another and this time it was to be brick, and the jailhouse with family quarters to live in would be of stone. A Barbourville contractor got the bid on this courthouse. In the meantime, a man named William Turner who owned most of the land which is Harlan proper, including some of the hillsides, offered to give one square acre of land to the county for the purpose of building a courthouse. The trustees waggled their heads and thought it was too far from town and it was in the middle of a cornfield; but a gift like this was too good to turn down, so the new brick was built where the present stone courthouse stands. The same contractor also was the successful bidder on the Presbyterian Academy which was built of the same kind of brick. The jailhouse was a two-story stone building at the south end of the courthouse with living quarters for the jailer. When the stone jail was torn down the stones were used at the corner of Mound and Second Street.

Felix G. Lewis and Henry C. Rice were appointed surveyors to lay off the land. Moses W. Howard was appointed to oversee the building plans. At that time expert builders were brought with the contractor and that is when the Gregory boys, Alonzo, Alvay, and Walter Z., came to Harlan. All the windows, doors, stairs and steps were made on the

Courtesy Harlan Daily Enterprise
Fourth Courthouse 1888

MOUNT PLEASANT, THE COUNTY SEAT

ground, according to Trigg Gregory, son of Alonzo. This building seemed to be adequate and it looked good with a cupola on top holding a large clock which nearly everyone in town could see. There was a plank fence all around the square which served as hitching posts when folk came to town, just as we park automobiles today.

Many of you can remember that the new stone courthouse was built in 1920. A jail was placed on third floor with living quarters for the jailer. The old stone jail was torn down, and I believe it was used in the stone house opposite the Harlan Hospital.

The earliest record I find in the County Court of Harlan is the marraige of Carolin McGeorge to Israel Nance, Feb. 26, 1818, by George Brittain.

The next record is James Hall to Sally Pace, March 20, 1818, by Preacher George Brother.

Thomas Ball married Rachel Kelly, March 9, 1820, by Galvin Bailey, preacher.

Isaiah Steely married Isabel Rose, March 2, 1820, by Elisha Green.

Thomas Forrestor married Sally Harris, March 14, 1822, by Galvin Bailey, preacher.

May Hall married Alexander Estep, March 21, 1830, by Samuel Howard, preacher.

William Turner married Stacy Smith, daughter of the Revolutionary soldier, Henry Smith, March 24, 1824, by John Lewis, preacher.

Charles Noe married Jane Dunlap, May 22, 1822, by Calvin Bailey.

Jemimah Lewis married John Jenkins, July 20, 1825, by John Creech.

Peggy Marks married William Benjey, July 21, 1825, by Elisha Green.

Sally Cornett married A. Holloway, Jan. 11, 1826, by John Lewis.

Robert Noe married Polly Forrester, July 22, 1826, Luke Noe, preacher.

Joannah Turner married Thomas Sowell, Sept. 24, 1827, by John Noe.

Milley Smith married Milton Greenbill, May 24, 1827, by Thomas Marcum, preacher.

Polly Taylor married Allen Hall, March 11, 1827, by Elisha Green. Allen Hall was the son of James Hall, the Revolutionary soldier and preacher.

Winston Huff married Stanny Parker, Feb. 12, 1827, Luke Noe, preacher.

Delia Noe named Peter Whitaker, Feb. 3, 1828, Jonathan Kelly, preacher.

John Clay married Elizabeth Farler, May 12, 1829, John Creech, preacher.

Thomas Huff married Catherine Morris, April 6, 1828, by John Creech, preacher.

William Coldiron married Leah Lewis, Feb. 20, 1830, John Dixon, preacher.

Sally Woolum married Barnabus Idol or Iclol, Sept. 12, 1830, by John Hendrixon.

Sally Creech married Isan Stenpar, March 20, 1830, John Dixon.

Samuel Howard, Jr., married Sarah Pace, Nov. 1, 1831, Elijah Green, preacher.

Jemimah Orsborne married John Helton, Jan. 5, 1832, by Samuel Howard.

Ezekiel Hall married Cloa Branson, March 7, 1833, by John Creech.

Jeremiah Forrester married Polly Orsborn, Aug. 5, 1836, Moses B. Evans, preacher.

Lucy Noe married David Fee, Aug. 7, 1837, John Noe, preacher.

The town of Harlan was called Mount Pleasant by the early scouts who came over the mountains from Virginia or perhaps by way of the Cumberland Ford (now Pineville) and found this small level spot nestling among the mountains like an inverted hat trimmed with ribbons of rivers and creeks flowing into the forks of Clover, Martin, and Catron Creek, converging at this place to form the head of the

MOUNT PLEASANT, THE COUNTY SEAT

great Cumberland River. Poor Fork and the creeks which flowed into it did not join the river until it reached a place about one mile from Mount Pleasant called Baxter. From the Pine Mountain side the creeks and branches that rushed down the hillside were said to be the best drinking water in the county because of the lime deposits which are not found in all parts of the county.

The town of Mount Pleasant was incorporated about 1876, so I have been told although I have not found a record of it, and at that time it was discovered that another place in Kentucky was named Mount Pleasant so by legislation the post office was changed to Harlan Court House and the town remained Mount Pleasant. People referred to it as Harlan Town or Harlan Court House until in 1912 it was incorporated under the name of Harlan. George Brittain Turner became the first mayor of Harlan and received his commission from Governor James B. McCreary. Elijah Lee Howard was city clerk, and W. C. L. Huff was police judge. W. W. Duffield was chairman of the Board of Trustees consisting of J. C. Brock. M. G. Ward, A. M. Clark, and the officers.

A copy of the resolutions was sent to Hiram M. Brock, then

Maston Green Ward, born 1868, later sheriff and jailer was son of Thomas Skelton Ward and Mary Francis Jones Ward. Her parents were Maston Green Jones and Sarah Lane Jones. He was the son of Johnny and Sally Noe Jones, son of the Revolutionary soldier, Stephen Jones.

Representative, later Senator. One of the first acts of the Council was to order a mud hole filled in front of the Presbyterian Church, provided the Presbyterian Church paid half the cost. John M. Middleton, former jailer, served on the council when they voted to build board sidewalks in the middle of town.

The post office address had been Harlan Court House and in 1878 when Sarah S. Buckhart Harris, widow of Captain Benjamin Harris, applied for widow's pension, her post office address was given as Harlan Court House, yet the town remained Mount Pleasant until 1912.

After the Harlan City Council began to function, they advised the people to keep the cows off the streets where they roamed at will.

The old frame courthouse is at the left of the brick courthouse which is in left center, right back is tower of the Methodist Church, extreme right is the frame Baptist Church. In the right foreground is the Presbyterian Church, Academy and Boarding Home, overlooking Clover Fork River.

The old frame courthouse was kept in use long after the brick courthouse was built in 1888. The old frame building was used for a Masonic Hall and other public meetings, and it stood near where the Christian Church and the A & P store are now. Across from them lived Henry Clay Rice and Sarah Amanda Eager Rice at the Mill-dam site, in the first frame house that was built in town although it has been torn down and the site is used for a parking lot.

M. Green Ward lived on the corner that is now Bowers and on the other side of the Rices lived Judge W. C. L. Huff. Later his son Hamp H. Huff and his wife Canna Hensley Huff lived in the big two-story Huff home and although they had no children of their own, they helped several of the Hensley and Huff nieces and nephews through school by keeping them in their home in town. This couple is now deceased but over a period of several years they helped educate fourteen young relatives.

On the other side of the Huffs lived a couple dear to my heart, S. J. Crittenden Howard, born 1845, died 1932 at the age of 86, and his wife Emily Ball Howard. He was formerly commonwealth attorney and a barrister, the son of Adron Howard and a descendant of the old soldier Samuel Hord. Mr. and Mrs. Howard had several children. The one I knew best is Elijah Lee Howard who now lives with his daughter, Imogene, and her husband Alga Christian. My own grandmother had died young, so when my parents wanted to take a trip, the S. J. C. Howards were good enough to take us children in their home and baby sit with us while our parents were away. Their children were really not much older than we were, but just enough older to be the right age to know how to treat and handle younger children. We loved "Mammy Critt and Pappy Critt" who used to entertain us with tales of bygone days. "Pappy Critt" told us many stories of the Civil War days and his childhood experiences with Indian boys who were still living at Wallins Creek where he was reared as a child, long before he ever dreamed of reading law. Both Mr. and Mrs. Howard had relatives on both sides in the Civil War and told us many stories of the war.

On the other side of the Critt Howards lived the George Brittain Turner family in a big colonial home where is now the Anderson-Laws Funeral Home. It was set back from the road with a nice big yard and beautiful shade trees. Their daughter, Nancy Turner, married Judge Moses Wilker-

23

son Howard and they lived there and brought up their family.

Across from them lived Fielding S. Hensley and his wife, Elizabeth Lewis Hensley. His widow lived in their old home next to the present service station across from the Presbyterian Church until she died at the age of 83 in 1933.

Will W. Noe married Margie Lewis, daughter of Judge Wilson Lewis, and lived on Second Street across from the courthouse and had their store and business on the corner of Central and Second.

Across from them on the opposite corner was an imposing building where Sam C. Howard and his wife Emily Smith Howard ran a hotel and store. The Southern Methodist Church was nearby and later merged with the Methodist Episcopal Church. The old Southern M. E. building was used for a schoolroom.

Will Blanton and his wife lived where Charles Chadwell Smith and his sister Sudie Smith now live on Second.

The old Baptist Church was near the present McDowell home on Central and across the street lived the preacher, where now lives Mrs. Mabel Morton. This is said to be the oldest house remaining in the town of Harlan. The Baptist minister was Randolph Browning who married Rebecca Howard in 1870.

Beyond the church east from Mound Street to Central and as far as the present schoolhouse was the colored graveyard.

James B. Smith, the first blacksmith in town, married Rissie Yeary and lived across from the present Carlo Cawood home on Mound Street.

Next to them was a widow, Mrs. Betsan Hall Langford, who kept roomers in a big two-story frame home. Next door to her on the west side was the home of Jeems Skidmore whose first wife was Jane Nolen. They had the first Graphophone in town and it turned cylinder shaped records and had a large horn amplifier. On warm evenings, they would place the Graphophone on the porch and folks from all over town would gather to listen.

MOUNT PLEASANT, THE COUNTY SEAT

There was no through street then from Mound to Ivy so there was no corner there at that time.

Sheriff Hamp H. Howard married Milly Carter and lived near the old Baptist Church on Third Street. She was the sister of John Bradley Carter and Molly Carter Nolan.

Radford Saylor, who married a widow Sadie Hensley Day, lived across from the Hamp H. Howards. Radford Saylor was a widower and his son is the well-known Rufus Saylor.

The Presbyterian Academy, Boarding Home and cottage for the Sunday school worker was on Clover near the junction of Clover and Central. Beyond the Presbyterian Academy, which also served as a church building, was the end of town, although several people lived farther east on the river bank.

Sherman Farmer who married Eliza Sergent had his home and repair shop near the church.

"Uncle" Bill Langford, who married Mary Lyttle, lived farther east and had a large family. Their daughter Susan married Nathan Osborne who was a practical engineer and an expert on drainage. Marge married Tom Fields, Stonewall married Ella Hall, Heinan married a Stanton, Shonn married Rosy Crider, Sarah married Alfred Harris and Dave married Mariah Middleton.

Alford Hall bought a lot on the river in the early days of Mount Pleasant. He married a Hall whose name was Sarah.

Near the Presbyterian Church lived John Ancil Ward and his wife Susie Brittain Ward. Near them lived David Hill Smith and his wife Susan Turner Smith, daughter of William and Minerva Turner.

At the corner of Third and Clover was the home of Judge William Floyd Hall and his wife Lucinda Howard Hall. Judge Jeremiah Grant Forester and his wife Jane Hall Forester lived at the corner of Third and Central. His brother, Judge James S. Forester, and his wife Mary Smith Forester lived on the opposite corner.

On Second Street near the courthouse was the stone jailhouse with quarters for the jailer's family. When I recall the jailhouse, John Metcalf and his wife Jane Creech Metcalf lived there. Next to the jail where there is now a service station was a boarding house run by Willie Creech who married Martha Blair.

Walter Z. Gregory with his first wife's family lived in the home occupied by Mrs. Carl Preston's daughter, Glyna Shoemaker Smith. The first Mrs. Gregory was Rella Turner, daughter of George Brittain Turner.

Jonathan K. Bailey and his wife Louisa Jones Bailey had their home and store near the present Gilly-Hoskins Furniture Company.

Joe Kelly who first married Mary "Pop" Rice-Hurst lived on Main Street near where the Brock Building is located, and ran a hotel.

John Jones, the merchant, married Martha Creech and they had their home and store at the corner where the Harlan National Bank is located.

G. W. Green had a store where there is a barber shop on the opposite corner.

Carlo Jones who married Ludie Turner lived between where Mrs. Henry Howard and the Roberts Motor is now.

Lafayette Harris had his home where the Baptist Church is now and he dug the first well in Harlan. The well was in the corner of the front yard about where the church steps are located.

Arthur Blankenship Cornett and his wife Ella Amanda Hurst Cornett had a home on the corner of Main and Mound. The old frame Methodist Church was almost the same site as the present one.

Henry L. Howard, one-time Commonwealth's attorney, lived where the parsonage is now and the brick in his home was made at the brickyard next door to the church.

Next door to the Henry L. Howards was the schoolmaster George Blackburn. After his death his widow and daughter "took in" sewing.

On the corner where O. B. Cornett lives was the home of Dr. William Turner Nolan who married Precious Cornett. He was the brother of the late Dr. J. W. Nolan who married Bertha Whitehead. Next door to them lived the widow

MOUNT PLEASANT, THE COUNTY SEAT

Malinda Johnson who operated the telephone office in her home. She was a sister of Mrs. Bill Nolan.

John Blair and his wife Rebecca Smith Blair ran the frame Harlan Hotel on the Bank-of-Harlan corner.

T. S. "Grandaddy" Ward lived where the post office is now.

There were several people who lived on the outskirts of town. The old Maston Green Jones place was where the Whitcomb Addition now is, and at the top of the hill lived Bony Crider and his wife and John Maupin and his wife who was a sister to Mrs. Crider. The Balls lived across the river—"Uncle" Albert Ball, George W. Ball and Robert Lee Ball. Milton Jones and his wife, the former Louise Turner, lived at what is now called Gilbert's Hill in Sunshine.

Toward Baxter there was a family named Uncle "Dow" and Aunt "Sook" Shackleford.

Cable swinging bridge over Cumberland River at Mound Street and Georgetown Park. Henry Howard, descendant of the Revolutionary soldier Samuel Hord. He was son of Nathan Howard who married a Pope. His brother Calvin Howard married her sister and several members of the family have red hair.

Up to this time, people who lived across the river from town used a canoe or flat bottom boat to cross the river and sometime after 1900 swinging bridges were built across the Clover Fork at Smith Addition and at Main Street. Over the Cumberland River there was a swinging bridge at Georgetown and one at the end of Cumberland Avenue to Huff Addition. There were swinging bridges built farther south at Catron's Creek and Martin's Fork. These bridges were held up by cables and accommodated only walkers, but there was a swinging bridge at Tremont which did accommodate a wagon and team. All the other bridges were near fords where wagon and teams crossed the rivers. The first steel wagon bridge was built across the river at Baxter and the next one was at Main Street which has now been replaced by a concrete bridge. Now there are very few swinging cable bridges left in the county because most of the roads have concrete bridges.

CHAPTER III

EARLY SCOUTS

WHEN the early scouts came into this section there was only a blazed trail from the western part of Virginia to this area. Many of the early families walked most of the way, bringing only what they could carry because the road would not accommodate a team of oxen. Occasionally an ox would carry a burden and once in a while a man could ride a steer. Not many of these early scouts possessed horses and mules. The scouts, spurred by thoughts of adventure, would spy out the land and return for their families. From some parts of Virginia and North Carolina a Conestoga wagon could be hired to carry the family part way. These wagons, built somewhat like boats, would float when crossing deep or swollen rivers; therefore they were not so apt to upset while crossing as were other conveyances.

The earliest mention of a survey is described as follows: "Lincoln County Examined and Recorded Book 14, page 550, fee 50 cts paid. Grant 600 Acres. Henry Lee Esq: Governor of the Commonwealth of Virginia, To all whom these presents shall come greeting: Know ye that by virtue and in consideration of part of a land office Treasury Warrant No. 10303 issued the 24 day of Dec. 1781 there is granted by said Commonwealth unto Christopher Acklin Assignee of John Latham a certain tract or parcel of land, containing six hundred acres by survey bearing date of 31st of March, one thousand seven hundred and eighty eight lying and being in the County of Lincoln on both sides of the South fork of the Cumberland River about three miles above the mouth of Cranks Creek and bounded as follows: to wit: Beginning on the South side, etc. thence to the beginning. With its appurtanances to the said Christopher Acklin, and his heirs forever. In witness whereof the said Henry Lee, Esq., Governor of the Commonwealth of Virginia, has hereunto set his hand, and caused the lesser Seal of the said Common-

Courtesy The Mountain Press, Gatlinburg, Tennessee

wealth to the affixed at Richmond on the 18th day of January in the year of our Lord One thousand seven hundred and ninety-two and of the Commonwealth the Sixteenth. By the Governor—Henry Lee, Secretary—A Copy Attest. J. A. Grant R.L.O."

In 1785 one Joseph Hoskins received Military Land Grant Warrant of 100 acres on Pucketts Creek.

An old McGavock Survey (also referred to as McGaffy) was a Revolutionary land grant which began at Meadows Creek on Catron's and was conveyed to John Carter and George Eager who married sisters, daughters of John Clark of Wythe County, Va. Once I saw a copy of this survey and I recall that it was signed by Patrick Henry who was governor of Virginia in 1785. He was the first governor under

statehood from 1776 to 1779 and again from 1784 to 1786.
An old census record gives the name of Nancy Bailey
Turner born 1785 near Evarts on Yocum Creek. She is
thought to be the first white child born in Harlan County.
She married John Cawood, son of Berry Cawood, the Revolutionary soldier, March, 1812. She was born 1785, died 1855
at Cawood, Kentucky, where she is buried.

Four young fellows, descendants of Revolutionary soldiers,
Left to right: Bob Cawood, Will L. Bailey, Carlo Jones,
Jerome Howard.

Samuel Hord came from Virginia and his son Wilkerson, called "Uncle Wix," was the first white child born in Mount Pleasant in 1792.

Jonathan Creech, father of Elijah and John Creech, migrated from North Carolina and came across the mountains through Virginia to the head of Poor Ford, at a place now called Benham. Benham was named for a group of campers headed by a man named Benham.

Everts was named for a family who lived there in the early days. One of the sons married the daughter of William and Elizabeth Cornett Campbell on Poor Fork.

Aley Ledford, born 1787, came from North Carolina to the place called Cawood. When the widow of Henry Smith, the Revolutionary soldier, applied for pension, he stated that he was her uncle, that his niece Betty Ledford married Henry Smith, Aug. 17, 1792, in South Carolina.

One of the oldest names in the county is Slater's Fork which was originally Slaughter's Fork. The Slaughters were from a long line of rectors in the Church of England. Robert and Francis Slaughter were the first church wardens at St. Mark's in Culpeper County, Va. Slater's Fork is near the head of Catron's Creek and was the first trail known to have been used by the white man.

Jemimah Pennington Smith testified that she knew Ephriam Osborne and that her brother Joshua Pennington was in the expedition against the Cherokee Indians and she understood that they were together in this campaign.

Jesse Brock, Revolutionary soldier, was the first white man to settle permanently at Wallins Ridge. He owned the land up to Fourmile Creek from Pine Mountain to Wallins Ridge.

Several of the Revolutionary soldiers stated in their application that they went as far as Herod's Station (Harrodsburg) in the scouting campaign.

Jonathan Kelly came across the Virginia mountains and settled at the head of Bailey's Creek, which was named for a party named Bailey. These campers went further down the Poor Fork River and when they returned next day, they saw evidence of a fresh campfire and the remains of some scouts around the fire and they never knew whether these men were killed by Indians and left to have their meat devoured or whether wild animals were responsible for their untimely end.

EARLY SCOUTS

Lewis Green, Sr., went as far as Fort Harrod as a scout in the Revolutionary War, and when he came back he surveyed over a thousand acres on the Cumberland River from the top of the ridges at Browney's (Browning) Creek to Pucketts Creek and purchased this land for about 5¢ an acre which was the cost of the survey.

The first Middleton who came into this county was Walter. It seems that his father died from heart failure on a buffalo hunt a few months before Walter was born, leaving him well-to-do. He started out in search of adventure and landed in Harlan County.

The Ball family came from Virginia and settled on Catron's Creek. They are said to be descended from the same Balls who are related to Mary Ball Washington.

It is said that the Cornett family came into this county because some men were trailing a band of Indians who had kidnapped a small white girl in Virginia. The little girl was recovered and after spying out the land, some of these men returned to Harlan County to settle.

Henry Shakleforte, a Revolutionary soldier, came into Harlan about 1801, according to his pension application.

Stephen Jones, Revolutionary soldier from Virginia, brought his family across the mountains to a place near what is now Verda. They stumbled upon an Indian hunting party, so they took refuge under a cliff by a creek which bears the name of Jones's Creek to this day. The family were too afraid to venture far from their shelter and for several days they ate buffalo scraps which the Indians had left at their deserted campfire. The Indians were so intent on their feast that they left without molesting the Jones family, although there is no doubt that the Indians were aware that the white people were there.

Berry Cawood stated in his application for pension that he came into Harlan County soon after the Revolutionary War.

Ephriam Orsborne, widower, was over a hundred years old when he died, Nov. 9, 1852. He said he served under Captain Enoch Osburn in the Revolutionary War. His son,

33

The Cawood (Keywood) family taken at memorial services at the grave of the Revolutionary soldier Berry Cawood. Among the descendants shown are Hiram Cawood and three of his sons, Green Cawood, Dr. William P. Cawood and Carlo B. Cawood.

Ephriam Orsborne, and wife "Polly" Mary conveyed a deed in 1857.

The John Murphy Wards came from Virginia and settled on Strait Creek in what is now Bell County. The Fusons settled on Pucketts Creek and the Lee family settled on Browney's Creek.

Thomas and Anna Hoskins were early settlers at Hoskins Ford in Bell County. There was a Thomas, Jr. George Burghart, a Revolutionary soldier, brought his family over the mountain from Virginia and it is said that he found the stump of a very large tree which was big enough to hold his family until a home could be built. He entered the service in Pennsylvania and no doubt they are of Dutch origin. The name is often spelled Buckheart, Buckhart and Burkhart.

In 1806 Dickinson, MacFarland & Company deeded some land on Poor Fork. In 1861 Boyd Dickinson's will was made in which he mentioned his wife Catherine T. Dickinson. This will was produced and recorded in the Harlan County Court June 25, 1886, by W. C. L. Huff, clerk. He appointed James R. Lloyd and Joseph Davidson his administrators and left his land to James F. Lloyd and in the event he lived longer than his wife his estate was to go to Joseph Davidson's and James T. Lloyd's children equally. The witnesses were proved in the Lee County Court of Virginia at Jonesville.

Some years ago C. G. Blair of Cumberland wrote an article in which he stated that Boyd Dickinson and his brother John made a survey and secured the patent to some 200,000 acres of land which he said was nearly all of Harlan County, at one time. He said that Boyd Dickinson, the older one, followed a wounded deer down the Poor Fork River to a place now called Dione. Here he encountered another party of surveyors who were surveying with the idea of securing a land patent from the government, and the Dickinson brothers, Boyd and John, were able to file their patent first.

Chapter IV

HOMES

BIG GAME was plentiful, such as buffalo, bear, elk, wild boars, mountain lions, wolves, panthers (painters or panters), and small game and fur bearing animals abounded, such as possum, coon, weasel, fox, muskrat, beaver, otter, coneys (rabbits), woodchuck, squirrels, geese, ducks, turkeys, partridges, perch, sun grannies, suckers, trout, catfish and eels.

The only beaten paths were to the watering places, usually called Licks.

After selecting a home site the scouts would help each other because it was not safe to travel alone. First they would build a crude shelter out of poles sort of teepee style and attach it to a large tree laced together with oak splits and bark. This

This is the house that Jack built in 1847, near Farmer's Mill. John H. Farmer married Rebecca Ledford, June 20, 1847, by Noble Smith, preacher.
In 1947 Ramsey and Jane Fulton Brock bought this home and restored and preserved it as much as they could. They have been living in it for fifteen years and as far as is known, it is the oldest building remaining in Harlan County. Turn to page 124.

HOMES

was used while the home was being erected. Any settlers nearby would join in and lend a helping hand. This was called a log rolling or log raising. A few men could practically build a house in a day. A homesite was always near a stream of water in a sheltered hollow instead of on a mountaintop. In passing by old homesteads people have wondered why they did not build on top of the mountain—the answer is water.

There was always danger in getting away from a campfire alone so it was necessary to find water close at home. These running streams were not always suitable for drinking water and when settlers located a good, cool spring they would carry the drinking water from it.

The construction of the chimney and hearth was the first step to building the home. The hearth stone and the arched keystone were carefully selected. The hearth stone was usually one large flat slab or more. A somewhat triangular stone was selected for the arch keystone. The side ends of the hearth were built like steps to hold vessels and keep victuals hot or warm. A few feet above the hearth stone there was a row of stone laid to jut out, thus making a fire board or mantelpiece. A mortar of clay and water was used to cement the rocks together. Certain qualities had to be found in the rocks also, because some kinds of rock split and break under hot fire. All the cooking would be done over a hearth fire except what was done over a bonfire outside.

The trees had been cut into logs and rolled into a place near the homesite. The dirt had been smoothed away to a layer of clay and sometimes the big logs were used for foundations instead of stone. In the beginning the sod or clay floor was used until a better floor could be made. In selecting the logs, allowance had to be figured for the chimney and the one door; no windows were used at first. There would be plenty of ventilation from cracks in the roof, through the chimney and when leaving the door open. Light would come from the fire at night and the open door during the day.

At the corners where the logs rested on each other crossed,

Courtesy The Mountain Press, Gatlinburg, Tenn.

about a foot was allowed beyond the corner and then each log grooved to let the log rest in the groove, thus dovetailing into each other. Cross beams were laid to support the loft and roof and the beams would be useful later to dry vegetables, by stringing them across the beams. Later a ladder, leading to the loft, would be made out of saplings and the beams would have saplings laid across them to make more storage space overhead and even for sleeping quarters. It was an excellent place to store apples, pumpkins, tobacco and other things. Saplings or split staves would serve as shingles called "shakes" to cover the roof which usually had two sloping sides. Then a mortar was used to chink the cracks between the logs. The door was the last thing to finish and

HOMES

Type of early log house

this was made of split logs pegged together with wood.

Later a puncheon floor might be added which was made of logs hewn off smooth and sanded by hand with stones. For the time being the clay floor would do although a little sand would be sprinkled on from time to time to keep down the dust.

The beds were bunks in one corner filled with leaves. Benches made of split logs and a rough table completed the furniture in the beginning. Wooden pegs for clothes and gun racks were driven into the green logs.

The only light was the firelight and daylight when the door was opened although a little light filtered through the dried mud calking and the roof.

It was desirable to have a large, long-handled iron spoon to stick into the clay mortar with a little "greece" poured into it with a piece of flax rag which served as an emergency light when the fire ashes died down.

The hearth fire was never allowed to go out even in summertime so that most of the old chimneys were in constant use from the time they were built until they were torn down. Some wood was always kept stacked in one corner so that a quick fire could be sparked in wet weather. These woodsmen knew their wood and they knew which woods burned quickly and which burned slowly. A slow-burning wood log was kept at the back of the hearth for a backlog and before that was consumed another replaced it so that they were always sure of stirring up the hot ashes to start a fire. Good resin pine knots were kept on hand for a ready fire.

Iron pots and vessels were coveted and were often traded or even stolen by the Indians. On their trek from Virginia everything was carried either on their backs or if they had dumb brutes, referred to as critters, the critters carried them.

Iron ore was used in the Alleghenies as early as 1608 and the first blast furnace was started by Alexander Spotswood in 1715 who served as governor from 1710 to 1722 under the Crown. A colony of German Protestants operated this furnace who were said to be experienced in iron works in Germany before coming to the Colony.

Every farmer knew some blacksmithing and could usually fashion crude implements out of iron pigots, which, though heavy, were easier to handle on a long trek than bulky finished cast iron. I do not know where they got the name pigot for ingot which was a brick of cast iron although I have heard that a Pigot family in England were iron-casters.

Iron pots, skillets and teakettles were the prized possessions. They were carried along on the trek to Kentucky because it was necessary to camp along the way and cook over campfires. Many of these early pioneers got sore feet from walking and had to go barefoot because shoes of that day were homemade and the shoe last was the same for each foot, that is, there was no right or left shoe.

Hardly a family came without a Bible and it is said of Dr. Thomas Walker that he would not travel on Sunday but spent the day meditating and worshiping God. Many families said prayers and recited psalms at the table and were said to be God-fearing folk. Some families possessed only a prayer book or Testament from which one of them would read aloud to the others.

Some of these families had a lot of plunder and where

HOMES

there were many helpers they were able to bring more items, even to flower seeds which were tied in a clean flax cloth to use later. Almanacs, copies of law books, slates, bed covers, feather pillows or beds, beaver hats, cowhide, buffalo hide, hemp, hemp seed, linsey, spinners, hand mills, iron, pewter and brass candlesticks, fire dogs, warming pans, knives, shovels, tongs, wolf traps, swords, pistols, guns, sickles, snuffers, tomahawks, ink powder, knee buckles, horn buttons, awls, wood piggins, lye soap, gourds, choice pottery and steel forks and sometimes a clock were among the articles brought to their new homes.

Nearly every family brought dogs with them and sometimes a cow and sheep were driven along with them. Some had oxen, steers or even horses and mules.

It is told that one woman had just set a hen with eggs when they decided to move, so she carried nest, hen, eggs and all in a basket all the way to Harlan County.

After the home was completed there were many other buildings to be erected—barns and sheds for the animals, woodsheds for cutting wood and storing during wet weather, storage cribs and fodder bins. The smokehouse to keep meat in was a much-needed building though many of the early settlers did not get to it for two or more years. Then a loom house was badly needed because there wasn't room in their one-room house for keeping the wool and setting up the weaving cloth. A flax board had to be made because all the clothing was made at home and it was as necessary as food and shelter. The flax was sowed on Good Friday or the nearest windless day thereafter, then it was harvested in summer, ripened on flax boards or breakers, left to ret and ted, and then the flax had to be beaten into thrashed fibers to form the linen thread.

Sheep were usually sheared after the weather got warm and it had to be washed, picked, combed, carded and rolled into yarn strings for knitting and weaving. Dyeing was an important part of the process so a loom house was almost a must with the settlers who usually had more to do than the day had time for.

Chapter V

FURNITURE, ETC.

THE women busied themselves with getting their new homestead in order while the men cleared land getting ready to plant a crop which consisted chiefly of corn, cane, hemp, oats, flax and tobacco. The pioneers early made a shelter ready for whatever animals they had, because sheep and cattle were necessary for food, clothing and leather, and were also used as beasts of burden.

The early homes did not boast a window but later some were added and it is said the early pioneer never cut a window larger than a deer skin could cover because there was no glass. A heavy shutter of wood was built on the inside and the skin stretched across the opening on the outside. Large strong wooden bolts fastened the doors and windows. The women were good at making things out of pliable skins, weaving baskets and getting the wool and flax ready to dye and spin and weave.

Meanwhile the men were making wooden vessels, iron and wooden implements, leather and wooden piggins and whittling bone needles and bone or horn buttons, combs and hairpins for the women. The line bone of the ham was considered the place from which to cut bone needles. A steel sewing needle was guarded like the slate pencil or gun.

Broom corn, sage corn, swamp grass and oak shavings were made into brooms. Some of the men could do this work better than the women because they were stronger and their woven willow and oak-split baskets were easier for the men to make than the women.

Oak splits were used to bottom handmade straight chairs and rockers.

The boys practiced slingshot targets and even with a pebble the boys could learn to down a bird at 100 feet in the air.

John Blanton Lewis, son of Felix G. Lewis, could usually beat any of the boys in a pebble-throwing contest.

FURNITURE, ETC.

Slingshots were made from a forked stick with a leather thong and the men folks took a lot of pains to make a good slingshot.

Matches were not common at this time and the men whittled sticks into squibs to place by the hearth so that a quick light could be ignited from the fire which was always kept burning. In fact matches were not usual to the backwoodsman until about 1880. They were known to "borry fiare" from a neighbor by carrying red-hot coals in a covered iron pot.

The furniture at this time was crude; so during the long winter months the men made furniture out of fruit and nut woods. The green wood was placed near the fire to cure and the men learned to make benches, chairs, looms, spinning wheels, chests and tables to an artistic degree. Small beds, cradles, trundle beds, cord beds, peg beds and high four posters were designed and made when the men had time to work on them. When extra company dropped in a pallet of covers was placed on the floor for sleeping and usually the boys were put on the floor.

In the late 1890's painted iron beds came into vogue and many of the old beds were discarded in favor of the new iron beds. They were fancy, having many curlicues and usually painted a pretty color. Then came the brass bed which seemed more elegant. Sofas were fashioned and placed in the "front" room which by this time was the parlor, and houses became larger. Long wooden benches with backs to them were used and sometimes called the "nussing" bench because the mother would sit in it and nurse her baby, while the next youngest would lie on the seat beside her and take a nap.

The old settlers counted money down to mills and it was probably after 1785 that the one-cent was common and they called it a "copper." The pound sterling was reckoned as the basis for money. Tobacco was considered as good as money although many items were exchanged or bartered.

In weighing measure, a "wait" was used as if it were an ounce or pound, that is nails, wax or lard would weigh heavy so a wait of nails would be an ounce. A "wait" of wool, linsey, feathers or tobacco would be reckoned as a pound.

Wax was used chiefly for affixing seals to documents. Nails were hand forged and used sparingly. Machine-wrought nails were not common until about 1830.

As late as the 1900's there was little money and the popular price was a shilling which at that time was reckoned at 16 2/3 cents in our money. Every bit of clothing, bedding and furniture was made at home as were most of the implements and utensils. Shoes were fashioned out of skins. Ground hog and cow hides were considered the toughest while deer, rabbit and weasel were softer and more pliable.

Wool was raised on the sheep and the housewife sowed the flax, and cared for it until it was spun into thread. Good Friday was said to be a lucky day to scatter the seed provided it was not windy, otherwise the wind blew it away. When the flax was ripe it was spread on flax boards to ret, rot, ted and cure so that the chaff could be beaten away leaving the lint fibers. Then the thread was ready to spin and weave into linens. Once when my little nephew came to the house in briefs on a hot day with no other clothes, I asked my father if his mother made their linen underwear for summertime and he answered "of course." He was born in 1858 and his mother was still weaving their clothes from linen, linsey-woolsey, or woolen material. The men usually sheared the sheep but the women washed, combed, carded, spun, dyed and wove or knit the wool into all the woolen garments that were worn. Then there was a mixture of flax and wool called linsey-woolsey which was not only durable but versatile.

The women took good care of their blankets and coverlids and when not in use they were folded and tobacco leaves placed between the layers with a few sprigs of lavender and sage as this was said to help keep insects away. All the old pieces of woven flax cloth were saved for bandages and for squares which would be used to tie up different kinds of herbs. The herbs would be placed in the middle, then the

FURNITURE, ETC.

square gathered up and a string tied around it to hang on a peg until it was needed.

Gourds were raised and cured for drinking vessels and the large bowl-shaped ones were used for salt, lard, grease, pumpkin butter, apple butter or milk.

Any housewife saved all the tallow and grease to use in making candles, lye-soap and for medicinal purposes. Cooking used up a lot of lard and tallow.

Potash lye soap was made from certain wood ashes and cooked together with grease and poured into vessels to cool and then it was sliced into soap cakes.

Drinking vessels, wooden butter tubs, called firkins, were made to hold butter, and wooden water buckets were called piggins. They usually had a leather strap to sling over the shoulder in order to facilitate toting it. Weggins were leather water bottles made from deer hide and sometimes held cider or wine. The top was gathered up with a strong thong, long enough for the leather strap to hang on a peg.

Sage, dried herbs, and seeds were tied in flaxen cloth and hung up to dry inside the house. Herbs were used for teas, stimulants, savoring, and medicinal purposes.

When the pioneer could locate a good water spring which was usually not very near the home place, he scooped out some dirt to form a small pool to provide drinking water. Branch water usually got warm in summer and a shady, cool spring seemed a better place to get drinking water. When the spring was very far away from the house, the women were not allowed to go without male help because of the danger of animals and Indians. I have seen springs a mile and a half from the house where the milk, butter and even eggs were kept cool. Some of the springs had a roof, shed and door built around them to keep anything from getting into the food. It is said that the Indians often stole in the spring and drank the milk or played tricks on the housewife by pouring the buttermilk in the water. The milk was kept in wooden vessels or clay pots or gourds. The butter was worked thoroughly with a wooden paddle to get the milk out of it so it would keep sweeter. The churns were wooden with a

45

dash stick and lid all made by hand. The lid had a hole in the middle big enough to push the dash stick through. The dashboard rested on the bottom of the churn and they poured in the clabbered milk, pushed and pulled the dasher up and down and after a while butter would form.

The women folk were very particular about keeping their milk-vessels clean by scouring them with sand and sunning them to keep the vessels clean and sweet smelling.

All the cooking was done on the fireplace except on occasions cooking was done on a bonfire or barbecue-pit outside. Outside the meat was broiled on a spit, especially if it was a large piece of meat. Inside it was usually fried or boiled, because they needed the grease for so many things and when cooked outside over a fire the grease was lost. Corn meal was the most staple food and it was prepared many ways. The water ground meal was a moist, coarse meal and many of the housewives only used water to make either a dough or a thin batter. One of the most common ways to cook it was called "johnny cake," which was a batter of meal and salt and water poured into a deep skillet which had been greased and heated in the coals. Then an iron lid which had a rim or collar of iron all around it was placed on the long-handled skillet and red-hot ashes and coals were placed on the lid which were held on the lid by the iron collar. In about an hour, this bread was crusty brown on the top and bottom and done all the way through. Sometimes the meal and salt was boiled in a large kettle and called mush. This was usually served with butter and molasses or sweetening. Maple sugar was short sweetening; molasses or honey was long sweetening. The scalded hoe-cake was a favorite with the pioneers. The meal and salt were scalded with boiling water forming a stiff dough, too hot to handle. Then huge spoonsful of this batter were dropped on a hot, greased griddle and turned over with a spade turner to brown on the other side. Pone bread or hobby bread was usually made with cold water and buttermilk with a little salt. The stiff dough was patted out by hand into hobbies or pones and baked in a hot skillet. This type of bread did not sour quickly and could be kept over

FURNITURE, ETC.

for another meal, if necessary. Bread was broken, not cut with a knife.

I am sure that the pioneers were not used to soda, the baking soda or baking powder that we have today because my grandmother used cream of tartar.

Green or unroasted was the only coffee available and indeed one did not always have coffee on hand. The coffee had to be roasted and then ground by hand. All spices, cloves, mace, cinnamon and pepper came in whole pods so that it had to be ground, pounded or grated.

Citron and pomegranates were raised something like gourd vines. Sage and lavender were raised in the gardens, dried and used as needed.

Paper was almost unknown; although it has been available to peoples for some centuries, it was not plentiful in the mountains. When going to a store or a house to swap goods, one carried his own container, a homemade sack, a woven basket, leather pouch or saddlebags.

Turkey wing dusters were usually hanging in every corner of the room because they were handy to tidy up with, and homemade brooms were used to sweep and scrub.

It was impossible to get a meal in the summertime without being pestered with insects, and a fresh, long limb or branch full of leaves was kept handy to brush away flies and other insects. This was called a "shoo-fly" branch. While the family was eating, someone would wait on the table and someone else would stand and wave the leafy branch constantly to shoo away the bugs.

Although the pioneers were not wasteful, they very often had no place to keep leftovers, especially in summertime so they were fed to the chickens or animals. They would say that there was some animal that would eat everything although some animals ate only a few things. My father did not like parsnips and he said that even "hawgs" wouldn't eat a parsnip.

CHAPTER VI

TOPOGRAPHY

THE first known party of surveyors, as the story goes, consisted of Wallins, Trace, Catron, Thranks and possibly more. As they emerged into an open place on top of the mountain, one of them suggested they scout around and decide which way to follow. The trail they had followed led from Virginia through McLin Notch and McLin Trail which is on the southern border of Harlan County, at that time part of Fincastle County, Va. Probably no one except woodsmen and scouts could have picked up this trail which led from Rose Hill, Va., across Cumberland Mountain at McLin Notch at a gap now named Trace Gap, going on to a place now called Pansy about seven miles from the county seat. The trail then turned westward across Black Mountain through a camping place, later named Wallins, and to a creek joining another creek which are now known as Pucketts Creek and Browning or Browney's Creek.

Earlier the only trail the scouts knew was through Cranks (Thranks) Gap to the mouth of Poorford or Poorfork at the place that is now Baxter. Possibly they discovered and named the creek called Martin's Creek. It was noted that this creek was much larger than Cranks which was named for a man named Thranks, but from usage is now called Cranks.

As this party of scouts followed the larger stream now known as Martin's Fork, they found that it converged with another stream, forming a T-shape. The lowland and meadows were so thick with cane brakes that they were impassable and people began to call this place Mount Pleasant. This convergence forms the head of the Cumberland River.

The creek was named for Catron when his party camped there for the night.

The names of these are almost proof that they were the first surveyors because the creeks and gaps still bear their

TOPOGRAPHY

Clover Fork and Martin's Fork meet to form the head of the Cumberland River, at Mount Pleasant. Logging men at work.

names. As they retraced their trip the following day, they crossed over at Pansy and followed the Indian path to an open spot which they called Camp Branch. There was plenty of water, snake weed grew thick and in the forest was game. Here they made their headquarters. Splitting up into two's or three's, they would return at night from looking around, and it was at this place that a tragedy occurred.

There are several versions of the story or account of Wallins' death. On their return to camp the other men saw blood on the snow and found the remains of him and his companion. Some say that Wallins' dog led them to his body while others say that his dog stood guard over the bodies, protecting them from wild beasts. At any rate these men had been killed by Indians and it is the first known death of a white scout to be scalped in Harlan County. The ridge where they camped, the creek and the town of Wallins were named for him.

There was another trail used by the early scouts which came through a gap called Benge. No doubt this was named for an Indian Benge who with his band made headquarters around Big Stone Gap. Here they crossed the mountain to another stream where clover grew abundantly and this stream is called Clover Fork.

Bailey's Creek was named for the leader of a party of men who camped on the banks of this creek. Bailey's party returned from scouting around and came upon a fresh campfire and there they found human bones, the only evidence left of some brave party who took off from Virginia. There lay their remains in this wilderness morgue. Wild animals were blamed for this tragedy; however, Indians could have scalped them and left them to the wild animals. There were signs of bear tracks around the blackened ashes of the campfire. This band of scouts told the story to other scouts they met and so the story of these skeletons being found is still told today. This was some years later than Dr. Walker's recorded trip where his party camped at Clear Creek Springs near Pine Mountain in 1750. This party made camp late on Saturday evening and being of religious nature they rested on Sunday. He said the water was good and that the laurel blooms were full. This places the time about late May. The next day they set out and came upon a good-sized river which Walker called the Cumberland after the Duke of Cumberland said to have been known as the "Bloody Duke." It is fitting that the festival held in Dr. Walker's honor at this place is called the Mountain Laurel Festival.

As more men followed the trails from Virginia into Harlan County, they left their mark with names of creeks, branches and hills. A woman named Polly Leddington Burgoyne gave the name Burgoyne to a branch which flows into Thranks Creek. Then Lick Branch, Jerry Branch, Bobs Creek, Cawood Branch, Crummies Branch, Little Branch, Turcle Creek, Rice Creek, Enoch Osborne Branch, Farmers Branch, Sugar Camp Branch, Little Grays Branch, Mill Creek, Dave Smith Branch at Tway, Daniel Skidmore Branch, all flow into the stream known as Martin's Fork which is joined by Clover Fork at the junction of Mount Pleasant, now Harlan. Trace Gap near Ligget, Slater's Fork (Slaughter) leads to the old Ford mines at Wallins. Then there are Pucketts

TOPOGRAPHY

Creek, Browney's Creek or Browning Creek, Hoskins Ford, Blacksnake Creek, Path Fork, Flat Branch, Saylor Branch, Jesse's Creek, Long Branch, Tom's Fork, Lee's Fork, Meetin' House Branch, Passin (Parsons) Branch, Rockhouse Fork, Cliffhole Branch, Straight or Strait Creek, Buffalo Branch, Rocky Branch, Wallins Creek, Forester's Creek, Terry's Fork, Hance's Creek, Cane Branch, Yeller Creek, Clear Creek, Caney Creek, Wasioto Branch, Fern Creek, Cubbage Branch, Devil Spring, Ball Branch, Camp Branch, Big Branch, Wattses Creek, Four Mile Creek, Flat Lick Creek, Salt Trace Branch, Laurel Branch, Nolan's Branch, Wido Branch, Frank Branch, Stony Fork, Jack Howard Branch, Reuben Branch, Chimney Branch, Middle Fork, Trace Branch, Bill Branch, Right Fork, Half-mile Branch, Sal Branch, Abner's Branch, Lick Branch, Goose Creek, Greasy Fork, Dave's Branch, Big Laurel, Little Laurel, Little Right Fork, Abner Lewis Branch, Alex Branch, Beech Fork, Dry Fork, Lick Fork, King Branch, Jake's Creek, Bear Branch, Line Fork, Ewing Creek, Meadow Creek, Hobbs Creek, Sang Creek, Banner Fork, Jones Branch, Baker Branch, Farmers Branch, Pounding Mill Creek, Big Branch, Crawford Branch, Mill Creek, Bard Branch, Coon Branch, Board Branch, Turner's Fork, White Oak Branch, Reed's Creek, Meadow Creek, Brittain's Branch, Razor Fork, head of Clover Fork near Lee County, Little Black Creek, Rock House Branch, Days Creek, Left Fork, Bryeden's Creek, Kelly Branch, Holmes Creek, Seagraves Creek, Middleton Creek, Mary Wynn Branch, Bear Creek, Lige Branch, Cracking Branch, Fugate Creek, Yocum Creek, Bailey's Creek, Jones Creek, Ages Creek, Gaves Branch, Shumate Branch, Lick Branch, Kitts Creek, Von Creek, Lin Holler Branch. On Big Black, Nolan's Branch, Looney Creek, John Lewis Branch, Zachariah Morgan's Ford, Jarret Branch, Huff Branch, Hensley Creek, Sargents Branch, High Bank Branch, Mags Branch, Lewises Spring and Smith Branch.

Gaps, Spurs, Rocks and other points are: McLin Notch, Cranks Gap, Grays Knob, Wallins Ridge, Salt Ridge, Salt Trace, Mayo Trail, Raven Rock, Hazard Gap, Rebel Rock,

Sukey (Sookie) Ridge, Johns Gap, Yates Gap, Shell Gap, Wolf Run, Laurel Break, Big Run, Ross Point, Goose Gap, Leatherwood Run, Benham Spur, Gross Knob, English Spur, Big Black Peak, Double Spur, Ewing Spur, Jesse Spur, Reynolds Mountain, Big Black Bench, Brittain Hill, Little Spur, Stone Mountain Peak, Brush Mountain Peak, Chestnut Flats, Grays Ridge, Little Black Peak, Looney Ridge, Sand Hill, Buzzard Roost, Indian Rock, Horseshoe Rock, Seven Sisters, Dry Ridge, Pace's Hill, Tanyard Hill, Hoskins Bench, Saylor Ridge, North's Run, Devils Roost, Wallen, Devils Back Bone, The Narrows, Wasioto, Kettle Island, Buffalo Run, Little Log Mountain, Big Log Mountain, Hangin' Rock, The Devil's Patch, Cumberland Gap, Big Cave (King Solomon or Cudjo's), Cold Spring Cave, Gibson Ridge, Sand Cave, Gun Powder Cave, Hagan Gap, Nigger Head Rock, Chimney Rock, Tackett Rock House, Aley Ledford Flats, Pope Mill Field, Pansy, Gilbert Holler, Gilbert Hill, Boogher Holler, Hangin' Holler, Hanted Holler, Lin Holler, Lovers Leap, Ivy Hill, Indian Cliff and Big Gum Spring.

All of these places tell a story although I have heard only some of them recounted.

The elevation of Harlan is 1,292 feet above sealevel in town and the highest peak in the county is the Big Black above Lynch which is about 4,173 feet. The Kentucky Highway Department has recently erected a road marker on the top where the road joins the Virginia line. Harlan County is approximately 484 square miles in area. It is oval in shape on the map and is from 15 to 20 miles wide and about 50 miles long.

The climate is varied with summer temperature running between 85 and 95 high and 55 to 70 low. In winter it snows several times a year and the days generally get up to 30 to 45 degrees and down to 15 or 30 at night. There have been a few extremely cold spells and in 1961 it got down to 10 below zero which is unusual. Windstorms, thunder and lightning are numerous but tornadoes are practically unknown.

Most of the rock is sandstone except in the Pine Mountain

TOPOGRAPHY

there is limestone and cave-like formation. The strata of the rock lies differently from the Blacks and Stone Mountain. Coal is the principal mineral, referred to as Black Gold and Black Diamond. Some of the seams are harder than others, and some are thicker than others. The rock formation on Pine Mountain is different from that of the Big Black and Stone Mountain; the rock strata is tilted.

Floods and rising streams have always plagued the settlers, especially when a deep snow is piled in the ravines and mountains. A warm rain melting the snow overflows the creek and river banks. Old folks told of a big flood which came shortly after the Civil War. Near Pineville at a place called the "Narrows" on the Cumberland River almost at the spot where there is now a motel, was a large two-story house which had been converted into a temporary hospital for wounded soldiers. The Narrows are steep, almost perpendicular banks and very high and at this time the water came over the banks. The water rose to the first floor of the temporary hospital and the wounded men had to be carried to the second floor. Then again about 1890 there came a cloudburst on Clover Fork and all the creeks came down with a rush until they said the wall of water was 75 feet high.

At that time the lumber business was the main industry in Harlan. There were three big lumber companies whose men cut logs and snaked them to the river banks awaiting high water to float them down the river. At Wasioto there was a log boom which consisted of many huge logs chained together to hold the logs until they could be separated by their brands. When the big wall of water rushed into Harlan, the lumber men got a fast runner to run through the mountain ridges to Wasioto to warn the people to get ready to save their logs. He arrived in time for the whistle to call in lumber men and they managed to take care of the logs. They had no telephone service.

The water is very good tasting in the mountains and is called free-stone water. There are small springs and wells that contain iron or sulphur and a little gun powder which are not good tasting. The iron and sulphur stain clothing and vessels but are said to be healthy.

Fishing was never done commercially in the county although before the railroad came in about 1911 the streams were full of varieties of fish. Many of the streams have been replenished with fish and every now and then you see a boy with a small string of fish.

Pheasant, partridge, turkey, ducks and geese are rarely seen although there has been some restocking by the Commonwealth. Once in a few years one hears wild geese fly over but on rare occasions.

Bear, buffalo, wolf, wildcat, deer and boar are almost extinct except that the state has stocked some bear and deer in this area. Bear and deer do not live well together and most of the deer that have been placed here wander to isolated areas.

Most of the choice lumber was cut when the lumber business was good here about 1890. Even before that the pioneers had used up a lot of timber. Mr. William Creech who donated land to the Pine Mountain Settlement School said that he guessed he had burned up $50,000 worth of timber in clearing land for crops.

Some of the clay in Harlan County was suitable for making brick although none was shipped out of Harlan as far as I know. There were two brickyards in the town of Harlan at one time. One was between the Methodist Church and Dr. W. P. Cawood's home and the other was where the Presbyterian Church stands. It is said that the chimneys of the old colonial home, where Mr. and Mrs. Moses W. Howard raised their family, were made at this site. It was next door to the Howard home which was originally the place where the Crumps had a log home.

Time was reckoned by the sun, moon, clouds and other signs. Suntime was used in this county until the railroad came in. Suntime was about halfway between Eastern time and Central and a native could tell you within a few minutes what time it registered. Everyone tried to get hold of an almanac and in those days they were usually sold and not

TOPOGRAPHY

given away for advertisement as they are today. An almanac was studied for all signs of weather and they gave some other information. All signs of weather were studied carefully and the stars, moon and clouds forecast enough to give the pioneers some idea of what the weather would fulfill. Once in a great while the Northern Lights could be seen in the northwesterly sky and some of the old people said the light could be seen from the great Chicago fire about 1872 when Mrs. O'Leary's cow kicked the lantern over and set fire to the barn which started the great conflagration.

Chapter VII

TREES

TREES played such an important part in the life of the pioneer that in modern times we can hardly believe how much the tree furnished for the benefit of the early settler.

When reconnoitering, the scouts climbed a tall tree to spy out the land and often used trees for lookouts and watchtowers. Shelters of poles, branches and skins were attached to trees for temporary camps.

All the first buldings were made of tree logs, saplings, shakes or staves for shingles. Oak and poplar were first choice on account of the durability and workability. All the furniture, most of the utensils, implements, plow handles, oxen yokes, sleds, gun racks, gun handles, pegs, pins and slingslots were all made of wood. Toy dolls and animals were whittled out of wood for the children and some of the men just liked to whittle for pleasure.

Property lines were marked by trees and many of the old surveys call for an oak stump, sweet gum, twin walnut, beech tree and so on until it is no wonder there have been squabbles over property lines, because time, man and weather have obliterated most of these boundary marks. Later rail fences were split and laid end on end forming a boundary line and at the same time serving to keep cattle inside the fenced property. This was a most laborious task and hardy men took many months to build these fences.

Trees also marked trails and paths that woodsmen could follow or otherwise might lose their way. Bees made their homes in hollow logs and even made their honey from the tree blossoms, and then the men robbed the bees for the sweetmeat and wax.

Many food-bearing and fur-bearing animals made their homes in trees and fed off the fruit, nuts, bugs, bark and saps from the trees. They also furnished protection and warmth for nests.

TREES

The better class of beds, tables, and other furniture was made from the nut and fruit and evergreen trees. Poplar was considered the best wood to scoop out a bread pan for mixing breads.

Trees furnished fuel for all their home fires and campfires and rich resin clubs furnished torches and flares when needed at night.

Trees furnished shade and also served as windbreakers for homes. They also furnished moisture for plants. The problem of crossing the rivers, branches and creeks was solved by laying long logs to stretch across the stream.

Flat bottom boats and canoes were made to paddle and pole across the deeper streams. Log freight and passenger ferries were constructed to cross the larger streams. There was a ferry at Cumberland Ford, Pineville, but I think it was built as late as the Civil War. Rafts of saplings laced together were used to tow packages which could not be placed in a canoe or boat.

Logs were used to improve roads wherever there was a mucky water hole; long logs were laid lengthwise and then a row of logs laid crosswise making what was called a cord road. Up until a few years ago there was the remains of the cord road on Boone's Trail near the old freight depot at Pineville. Weapons such as curved sticks, clubs somewhat like the shillalah (shillelagh) made from a twisted root could wield a wicked blow. Canes and walking sticks and fishing poles were made from long slender limbs. A torch resin club or light would often scare away animals.

Fowls and turkeys and birds roosted in trees and could be easily found by the pioneer. The bark, root and leaves furnished the basis for homemade remedies and potions, lotions and dyes.

The sugar maple was tapped to bleed the tree of sap which sap was boiled in large vats and made into syrup and sugar. This method today is used in some parts of the mountains.

Trees made the axle that was turned to crush the cane

which was boiled into molasses or sorghum. A long wooden paddle was used to skim off the foam as it boiled.

The service tree (called Sarvis) was supposed to have received its name from soldiers who picked the berries when scouting for war parties. Old people say the Civil War soldiers found this berry very useful in eking out their poor forage. It is also a tree with nice foliage and pretty, dainty, white, roselike blossoms which blooms before many of the forest trees bloom, sometimes as early as April.

A cold spell of weather always comes about the time dogwood blossoms are in bloom and then about the time the blossoms shatter. This is referred to as Dogwood Winter and it often frosts during this cold weather. In the fall the berry of the dogwood is quite bright red and the leaves begin to turn in late summer so that they are almost as attractive in fall as in the spring.

There is a legend about the dogwood that at the time of the Crucifixion the dogwood had been as large as the oak and so stout that it was used for the cross and forever after the dogwood has been dwarfed into a bent and twisted small tree. The petals of the blossom form a cross and at the outer edge they are rust-stained with the blood of Jesus and in the center is a tiny crown of thorns. The wood of this tree is beautifully white and can be made into small chairs which are nice.

The red bud is a native tree with beautiful, tropical-like leaves and a rose-lavender blossom like a tiny bleeding heart. It is said that when Judas went out and hanged himself that he happened to use a red bud. At that time the blossoms were said to be a pure white that clung in little drops to the branches. Then as Judas died his blood stained the blossoms and forever after they have been a purplish-pink. This is often called the Judas Tree and because it is one of the first trees to show blossom in the spring it has also been called the tree of life everlasting symbolizing the Resurrection of Christ after his death on the Cross and the Crucifixion on Calvary.

There is the story that the holly was used to torture Christ with the crown of thorns which was made from the holly leaves. Ever since that time holly has been used in connection with Christmas because of its red berries and thorny leaves.

Then there is the hawthorne which is associated with the Bible. It is said that Joseph of Arimathea went to England on a pilgrimage and when he stopped to rest he stuck his shepherd stick into the ground and it burst into white blossoms. It is known as the hedge-thorn or hawthorne and bears a small red fruit called haws.

The oak tree has a legend that at one time its leaves were evergreen but during the Crucifixion of Christ that all the other trees bowed their branches in grief, but the proud oaks would not bow so they began to lose their leaves. Their leaves do drop off now although they cling sometimes until the March winds tear them away. The bark was boiled to make dye. Its wood has many uses because the wood is strong, hard and durable. When white oak was used for kitchen tables the wood could be scrubbed with sand stone until they were nearly white.

Any of the nut family furnished food for many animals but the acorn was the favorite of the hog. The hogs were allowed to run in the forest to fatten on the nuts in time for winter slaughter.

The locust is another tropical-looking tree which has a beautiful white globule-shaped blossom with an almost too sweet odor. There is a rare variety which is a beautiful pink in color. The bark of the locust is rough and the wood resists rot. It was used a great deal for cord wood roads and when wire fencing came into use, locust made the most lasting posts. Moreover, the green posts sprout easily and often formed a live fence. The leaves are quite small and fern-like. It is often called the honey-locust and honey made from the flowers is almost pure white.

The pawpaw tree is a most interesting bush with large leaves that produces a fruit called the Kentucky banana. It is a sweet, tropical-like fruit which gets ripe in the fall, is about the size of a sweet potato and gets very soft and squashes when it hits the ground. The skin is green, turns yellow as it ripens and as it gets more ripe turns almost black on the outside, but the meat and pulp resembles a ripe banana, especially an over-ripe banana.

The buckeye tree is a native tree and very early the settlers found that the young tender leaves in the spring were fatal to cattle if the young sprouts were eaten. The nut of the buckeye is considered poison to eat and as far as I know nothing eats them except the squirrels. Instinctively the squirrels know that part of the meat is good and the little busybodies know which is not poison. The first buckeye you pick up in the fall is considered a good-luck omen. This tree was named by the Indians because the nut resembles the eye of a buck. In their poetic way they called it Heituck. The wood is light weight and easy to handle and is said to be good for putting up temporary sheds and the like. It was good for light utensils such as bread trays, spoons, sap ladles, boat paddles and many other items. The buckeye wood does not burn easily so that it made a good backlog for the fireplace. The flowers of the buckeye are quite pretty and come early in the spring for the bees to gather honey.

The sycamore is another tree associated with the Bible. There was the rich Zacchaeus who was small in stature and he climbed a sycamore tree to see Jesus. When Jesus came close enough to speak he told Zacchaeus that he would visit him that day. Zacchaeus was surprised and pleased that Jesus would notice him. Our old patriarchs revered the sycamore and found many uses for it. It is a quick growing tree with a maple-like shaped leaf which makes good shade. Another name for it is the button tree.

The weeping willow is a popular tree for shade but the switches were brought from Virginia. It is said that John Park Custis who was George Washington's stepson received the original switch which was presented by a British officer from England. It grows easily in this climate.

There is a legend of the mountain roses or wild rose as it is sometimes called. At one time the rose tree was quite large and a little girl shepherdess watching the Wise Men bearing gifts to the Baby Jesus wept because she had no

TREES

suitable gift to carry to Bethlehem. The rose tree knelt down to comfort the little girl and its petals changed from white to a delicate shell pink and to this day the wild rose kneels with its graceful fronds and does not grow to be a tree.

The ailanthus or tree of heaven is very prolific in these mountains and the odd thing is that it is not native. About one hundred years ago a politician introduced the tree and at first it was used for decorative shade because it has a bright orange tropical-looking blossom. In the summer they have an irritating, feathery waste which is wafted along on the breeze and lands everywhere. The leaves are sort of frondlike, and the wood is very porous; in fact one old man said it wasn't even good for fire wood. It has a cluster of beans that are inedible, and these seeds spring up and spread.

The story of Johnnie Appleseed is almost a legend but I think he really existed because they called him John Chapman. In this new country the apple tree was longed for by the settlers as were other kinds of fruit trees which did not grow wild so every time someone went back to Virginia, they tried to bring seeds back with them. Johnnie Appleseed traveled a good bit and he started out by filling his pockets with appleseeds. These seeds he would give to everyone he met as a good will offering and it is said that his seeds are growing all over the Ohio River valley.

Christmas was not celebrated with trees set up in the homes as we know them today. When I was a child, each church would have a large tree which was beautiful with real tiny candles and people exchanged gifts under the tree at a Sunday school entertainment. It usually took at least two men to stand guard to watch the flame of the hot candles for fear of starting a fire. I do not know when the churches began to use Christmas trees but I think it was late 1890, because it was introduced into England by German Prince Albert when he married Queen Victoria.

It has been said that Martin Luther started decorating Christmas trees in the home. He was out walking one cold, crisp night when snow was on the ground with frost glistening, the stars were pink-fire in the heavens and peeped through the tree branches which were evergreens covered with snow. It made him think of Heaven so he took the thought back to his home and cut an evergreen to trim with lighted candles to keep the thought of Heaven at Christmas time.

The wild crab apple was much used for its pungent taste and in later years when jelly making was learned, everyone tried to get hold of crab apples to make jelly. It is said that the crab apple was at one time very sweet and a little girl was trying to reach the apple when she accidentally broke off the limb of the tree which held the apple. This made the crab apple tree very crabbed so from then on the crab apple was very strong and puckery.

The hickory tree, besides furnishing nuts and wood for furniture, was the wood used in making a slow fire to smoke bacon, hams and sausage. The meat was strung on rafters over the fire and slowly cured, thus drying out the water, forming a coating which helped to keep away bugs and insects. Another name for it is the butternut tree.

The wild cucumber is a species of magnolia and looks quite tropical. The Indians called it wahoo because the cone shaped pod was sometimes tinged with red or fire color. The blossoms are very large, creamy wax-colored. It has a very large deciduous leaf and I recall that when we were small we used to gather these huge long leaves and lace them together with twig pins and make hats, skirts, and aprons. The blossom has a very strong, pungent odor and is almost overpowering when brought into the house. It grows in woodsy, clifflike places where the soil looks rich and covered with many dead leaves and in moist looking soil. Sometimes it grows along shady creek banks and when the big petals fall it leaves a cone, shaped something like a cucumber.

The persimmon tree is another tropical-like fruit which is native. The fruit is very sweet, and like an apricot is pink and luscious. If pulled and tasted before it is ripe it puckers the mouth like alum. After the frost touches the fruit it drops off the tree and becomes soft to the touch and has a

TREES

piquant flavor. Bears are said to be very fond of persimmons. When hunters went out for bear in the fall, they looked for a persimmon tree for there they were sure to find a bear.

The mulberry tree is another tropical-like tree with heavy dark foliage and a too-sweet berry, shaped somewhat like a blackberry, except that the berry is more purple. Many adults are afraid to eat mulberries because they have been sick from getting spider-egg poisoned from berries where the spider lays it eggs. For that reason it is not a popular fruit in the mountains. The mulberry is or rather was cultivated in the old countries for the raising of silk worms that spin their cocoon on the mulberry leaves.

The tulip tree is another tropical-like tree commonly known as poplar. It is very beautiful when in blossom and is alive with bees gathering honey during the blooming time. The honey made from this bloom is dark in color and has a sharp, piquant flavor. The poplar wood is very strong and durable and makes beautiful furniture and in building, the poplar is very resistant to rot.

The lin tree, or basswood or linden tree, is lovely with cream-colored flowers. It also looks tropical and the bees produce an almost pure white honey from the bloom which is considered the finest honey in the mountains. This tree is suitable to make light-weight utensils such as bread trays, paddles, oars and many other things.

The sourwood tree has flowers that produce a sharp, pungent honey. It has pretty foliage in the fall. The old natives thought enough of it to name a fiddlin' tune "Sour Wood Mountain." It has many verses and the singing fiddler usually made up verses as he fiddled along. One line is "Chickens crowing in Sourwood Mountain, Hey-diddle-dee day," and so on.

The black walnut was one of the most liked of the trees. In the fall nuts would be cracked out for food and some stored away to be used during the winter. Every farmer wanted a walnut grove and each year usually planted all he could spare. The wood makes up into furniture with a beautiful glossy, satinlike finish, and dark brown dye is made from the walnut hull.

. The chestnut was a beloved tree which produced both nuts and wood. Some twenty years ago a blight killed all the native chestnuts although I understand there are a few young trees coming on. The reforestation experts advise planting an imported chestnut now which is resistant to blight.

The hemlock tree is one of the cone-bearing evergreen trees and in some stages of its growth the leaves are very poisonous. Up until a few years ago, there was no known antidote for its poison. Socrates, the old Greek, is said to have used the hemlock in his cup of potion for his tragic ending.

All the evergreens were used for fuel, resin torches, furniture and even the foliage made a good base for bedding until the housewife could get together enough feathers for bedding.

The cedar is a stately tree of the evergreen fir family, bearing cones. It grows to great heights and is thought to be similar to the kind that were used in Biblical times referred to as the Cedars of Lebanon. The wood is fragrant, resists vermin and was prized in making closets, chests and storage drawers. It is often called red cedar due to the reddish color of the wood.

The laurel tree is really a shrub and not a bush but it has a beautiful pale pink bloom in May. It seems fitting that the Mountain Laurel Festival, in honor of Dr. Thomas Walker, is observed during the month of May. Annie Walker Burns, a genealogist, organized, promoted and started this festival with the help of citizens of Bell County. The leaf of the laurel tree is rich and waxy green all winter and it makes a nice yard shrub. The laurel leaves were called the victory laurel which was used to crown the athletes. In our native lore we called the laurel-shrub "ivy" which is not correct. Here in the town of Harlan there is an Ivy Hill and an Ivy Street named for this shrub which grows abundantly, but this shrub actually is the laurel bush.

While the rhododendron is not a tree, it grows to be

quite large with flowers that generally are a blush pink. Legend has it that the purple rhododendron used to have pale pink flowers. It seems that two young Indian boys were ambitious to become strong Indian Braves and while practicing the art of scuffling somewhere near Cumberland Gap, one of the lads lost his footing, rolled over a cliff and his body lay broken and bleeding in a clump of rhododendron trees. The pale pink flowers turned to a purplish-pink from the blood of the dying boy and forever after there have been purple rhododendron flowers to remind the Indians of the young boy who fell to his death because he wanted to be an Indian warrior. This purple variety is found in our mountains but it is not as common here as the blush pink.

Chapter VII

ANIMALS

ANIMALS, both wild and tame, had a great influence on the lives of the early pioneer. The domestic animals consisted of cattle, stock, both horses and mules, sheep, goats, fowls, hogs and dogs. A farmer in those days had to be a veterinarian, and when an animal got sick any of the nearby neighbors would lend a helping hand.

In the early 1800's horseracing was quite a sport and horses were not used for working as much as mules. Mules were more sure-footed on the hillside and could pull a loaded wagon better than horses. Mules were notional and would work perfectly willingly for one man when another man could not handle them at all. Mules took notions about certain harness mates also and would often work better with a horse than another mule. In other words a man had to understand a mule to get the most work out of him.

Sheep needed care and since a farmer had not the time to be a shepherd, he usually tried to get a dog which was good at taking care of a flock of sheep. I do not know when the German shepherd was imported to this country, but it was considered the best breed to train for a shepherd dog. The shepherd dog could also be trained to bring the cows in from the pasture. Sheep were absolutely helpless if a wolf got into the flock and while the older ones could run pretty well the lambs were sitting ducks. Lambs were a great care to the farmer because the lambs were born during the cold late winter and often the mother ewe died a-lambing and the little lamb had to be brought inside to raise. Usually these small lambs were brought into the house and one of the children was given the lamb to care for and feed.

Goats could pretty well look after themselves but were not as useful to the farmer as the sheep. In the early days the fowls were left to roost in trees and lay their nests where they could until a chicken house could be provided. Hogs

ANIMALS

were let roam over the forest to forage for themselves. However some hogs were kept around the house and a pen was made of stone because the hog could root right under a log fence. Most farmers made an enclosure at one end of the home because hogs are natural enemies of snakes and it is said that they will kill any snake and eat it too.

The wildcat sounded almost human. Especially at night he cried like a baby, screamed like a woman and the sound was eerie enough to scare the bravest man. The wildcat, often referred to as a varmint, was almost as much feared by the early pioneer as the bear and wolf. The cat was called many names: mountain lion, painter, panter, panther and mountain cat. Horses were skittish when they sensed a wildcat because a wildcat would jump a horse or cow and often mortally wound it. The cat would watch a traveler from a high vantage on a slanting log, rock, cliff or tree limb and be ready to spring on the victim. The hunter was alert also and a mule or horse could sense a cat before man could. One old man said he was alone one day in the woods and sat down to rest on a log but his gun was loaded and ready to fire. Some slight sound caused the man to raise his eyes and a huge cat was springing in the air, but the man pulled the trigger and felled the cat just in time to save himself. Some of these mountain lions grow to about two and a quarter feet and weigh more than a hundred pounds.

In the fall of the year several men would get together to hunt meat to cure for the winter. The hogs roamed at will in the forest so they had to be shot and killed. A wounded hog is dangerous so it took a good, steady eye and hand to kill the hog; too, its hide is tough and it is not easy to strike a vulnerable spot. A long, heavy gun was used which was known as a hog rifle.

The carcass of these animals was carried to the nearest home where all the men helped skin, cut up and divide the game in equal shares. This kind of slaughter was called a Batwahr. In the earlier days a high log pole was set on two erected cross logs about twenty feet up so that a wolf could not jump for the meat which was strung along this pole to cure for the winter. Otherwise the wolves would rob the family of their meat.

Dogs were the real friend to the early settlers. Several kinds of dogs were needed, the hunting dog which could tree a coon, the hound which could catch a fox, the bird dog which was needed for fowls because a baying hound would scare away the fowls. A sheep dog or even two were needed to watch a flock of sheep. And there was the watch dog for the house which would bark at a hawk, weasel or scare away even a bear. It is said that a tiny dog will keep a bear away from the garbage can because a bear hates a dog as much as he fears the man-scent.

A traveler once told of going to a mountain home to spend the night after a hard day in the woods checking out some timber. The owner of the house told him he was welcome to stay and he would feed him and give him a bed. When they got ready to retire the host said that there were snakes in the loft. Pointing to his old dog Red he said, "Don't you worry nary bit. Old Red will jump a snake afore he hits the floor."

Once someone gave my father a trained dog named "Rattler," which had been trained to kill snakes. My father built a home on a hillside where no family had lived for about fifty years and he thought it was a good idea to have a dog on the place. He was white and must have had some bird dog in him though he did not look like one. He had been trained to catch a chicken by the owner pointing one out in the flock and he never bothered any other chicken, but would bring that particular one in. Before the days of refrigerators people caught, killed, dressed and ate chickens the same day, so it was hard to run down a chicken if you needed one in a pinch. People thought fried chicken was the finest meat you could serve to a guest and guests came unexpectedly in those days because there were no telephones.

This same dog, Rattler, was with my sister one day and she was not within sight of the rest of us where we were hoeing corn. She came bringing in a woodchuck which she and the dog had caught and she had killed it with a club.

ANIMALS

My father was very excited about it because he said that a groundhog is dangerous when cornered, and although they look sluggish, sleepy and clumsy any wild animal bite is likely to cause infection.

My mother cooked this groundhog in the proverbial way and served it with sweet potatoes but I don't think any of us relished it very much because we were not used to wild game and the meat is very rich and greasy.

My father got the first Jersey cow in the town of Harlan and it was a scrawny and sorry looking sight when it arrived. He bought it at London, Ky., which is a distance of about 172 miles; at that time he had to go that far to buy goods and haul it back to Harlan. This young heifer had to be driven through on foot and it lost a lot of weight and was smaller built than the cows which most of the farmers had here. When all the men came out to look at it my father was "plagued a sight" on account of the way they teased him about his fine Jersey heifer.

The Indians taught the mountaineers how to catch a snake alive with a forked stick and many of the mountaineers carried a forked stick with them in the woods. When they would see a snake they would push the forked prongs over its neck and hold the head from striking at them. They used to bring live snakes into the county seat just to show them off but first they built a small cage to hold them inside. I have never heard of any bounty being paid on snakes but it seems to me that they were dangerous to the pioneer and certainly they were more numerous generally than they are now. It is said that the Indians would kill, skin, cook and eat rattlesnake meat. They used the skin for decoration to show their prowess.

Except in superstitious sayings, I have never heard a reference to the tame housecat during the old days, although they are plentiful now. It was common for farmers to allow black snakes to stay around the barns and cribs to eat mice and small rats. It is also said that a black snake will fight and kill poisonous snakes. I have heard my father say that Granpaw Green kept black snakes around the barn even though he and his brothers were afraid of snakes and dreaded to go to the barn although they had to help take care of the stock and get corn from the crib. If one of the boys did kill a black snake they would never admit which one it was because Granpaw would punish the one who did.

Bees were a real help to the farmer in supplying their long sweetening. Long sweetening was the name for honey and sorghum while short sweetening was maple sugar. The bees were cultivated from wild bees. After the farmer captured the queen bee from a swarm of bees, he would bring in the swarm and put it in a homemade hive which was a hollow log with a floor at the bottom and a lid made for the top. Obviously the farmer had to know something about the habits of bees. I have helped my father hive bees and there is danger from getting stung, particularly when the bees get confused, hot, bothered and angry. Usually a cool evening or the early morning is the best time to work with bees.

Bears are very fond of honey and many of the old pioneers would come upon a wild bee hive which had been robbed by the bears. It is said that if too many bees get after a bear he will run to the nearest water and wallow in it.

The bedtime story one old man told his young fry was about his grandfather who when a young lad was out cutting timber in the woods one day when he saw a young brown bear cub. Thinking that it would be a nice pet to take home with him, he picked it up and about that time the cub's mother broke through the bushes, lunged at him which scared him into dropping the cub. But the mother was not satisfied, and she came right on after him. She was angry and he knew he could not outrun her so he ran to the nearest tree and climbed up out of her reach till she left.

When everything seemed calm, he got down out of the tree and ran for home. Later they tracked the bear and brought the cub home to the children to raise for a pet. But a bear is never a satisfactory pet; they seem rompish and playful when little, but they are wild and often become unruly.

Bears can climb a tree better than a man, but they are so

ANIMALS

heavy and clumsy that they are afraid of a limb breaking and dumping them to the ground. They can move swiftly in spite of their clumsy look, so it never paid a man to get within clawing distance of a bear because one can lay his ribs bare with one stroke of his cutting claws.

It is seldom that bear and deer are found in the same part of the forest. The deer avoid the bear and will walk for miles to get out of a bear's habitat. They are swift and can outrun a bear, except for their young which they will not desert.

The hunters felt the greatest conquest when killing a bear of all the animals although they were proud of any of their hunting success. They talked a great deal about bear tracks and of seeing a bear going in a certain direction, but when a hunter came within sight of a bear, especially face to face, he became so excited that often he could not pull the trigger. The same experience came to them when they sighted a big buck and this overeagerness caused a nervous shake which was known as "buck fever," "buck ague" "buck eager," and it was no joke. All the hunters acknowledged that they would get the buck eager at some time or another when in the woods. There were times when they would shake so they could not reload a gun and at that moment might be the time for the back-end man to have his reward by getting his bead in at a safer distance.

The bear was much feared by the pioneers, but they did not bother in the winter because that is the hibernation period. In the fall of the year the bear is fat on nuts, berries and favorite tidbits and is not feared at that time as much as any other season. This is the season the men organized hunting parties to go for bear. The fur skin of the bear was prized for robes and rugs and the meat was eaten very much like pork. The meat is fat and oily and is stringy and tough, but that was before the days of milk-fed beef. The young are born during the hibernation period and it is said that they are no bigger than a mouse at birth. When the den mother comes out in the spring of the year is the most dangerous time to encounter a bear, because she is hungry, food is scarce at that time in the mountains and she is in no mood to be reckoned with then. Too, her mate often accompanies her for forage and even if you see only one bear the other is likely to be somewhere near.

The mother doe will use almost any subterfuge when she thinks her young are in harm's way and even the buck will often deploy the attention of man to distract him away from the female deer. Then he tries to outrun the hunter. They are wild, but can be tamed when young and become as easy to feed as a calf. There is a story told of a woman who was washing clothes on the river bank at Straight Creek when suddenly a young deer jumped right in front of her. She was so surprised and startled that she was stunned for a moment but not too much to hit and kill the deer with her batting stick. The batting stick was a wooden paddle which was used to beat the dirt out of clothes.

It is said that a duck and drake will mate for the season and they pay no attention to any other ducks while they are raising a family of ducklings. The one drawback about raising ducks and geese was the water stream. If the ducks and geese get in the branch water they follow it to the river and once they get on the Cumberland River they are likely to go as far as Barbourville. They were so important in furnishing food and feathers that most farmers looked for a spring on their land to dam up with earth so that water could be furnished for the ducks and geese and would not be connected with the little waterways. Geese mate with a gander for life and if something happens to either the goose or the gander then the other remains alone as long as he or she lives. My father was given one of these lonesome geese once when we lived in town and it followed him everywhere he went. He couldn't even go to the post office without this goose following him. Everyone in Harlan town had barns then and the poor goose had a place to stay but was lonesome.

A crow would also make a great pet although the crow was an awful nuisance to the farmer because his beady eyes could see corn grains through the dirt. A crow can be taught to talk although I could never understand what it says. There was a woman who owned one and had made a pet of

ANIMALS

it and she said it liked bright, gleaming objects. She had one piece of jewelry which was a gold brooch that she kept on the mantelpiece—usually called fire board. She missed the pin one day and thinking someone had accidentally knocked it into the fire, she took out the ashes carefully trying to find it. Some months later a member of the family saw the crow pick up a piece of metal and fly to the forks of a tree and hide it. Later they went to the tree and there they found a cache where the crow had been hiding little treasures for himself and among these pieces was the long lost brooch.

Hawks were always a menace to the chickens and it was hard to scare off a hawk where there were little chickens. The hens would cackle, the dog would bark and the people at the home would run out and wave their hands trying to scare off the hawk, but sometimes it caught a little chicken. Most farmers kept guinea hens around the place not so much for their meat which is quite dark although good enough to eat but because the guineas are such good alerters. When they see someone or something unfamiliar coming near they set up a plackety-plack racket until some member of the house comes to see what is the matter. Their eggs are good and look more like a bird egg than a chicken egg.

The eagle was at one time a menace to the farmer because it could swoop down and pick up a hen and carry it away right before your eyes. It has been told that the big bald eagle which often had a span of seven feet would carry off a little lamb or even a calf.

The county offered bounty for many kinds of predatory animals, and it is only once in a while that you hear of one of these animals being seen in this county. Bounty: $7 for eagle, $6 wolf, $5 bear, $3 panther, $2 weasel, $2 fox, $1 wildcat, $1 groundhog.

CHAPTER IX

PEOPLE, ANCESTRY, NEGROES, ETC.

THE early pioneers of Harlan County were predominantly of Anglo-Saxon descent, mostly English, Scotch, Irish, German, Dutch and French. A few Negroes were brought along with these early settlers and helped many families make a home out of the wilderness. Most of these pioneers were from families who belonged to some type of protesting Christians. There were followers of Friends, Quakers, Knox, Wesley, Calvin, Luther and leaders whose names have probably been forgotten. The French seemed to have come from people who became Hugenots during the Reformation period and family names such as Arnett, Branson, Colette, Codelle, Brummet, Cornett, Cope, Farler, Felices, French, Fultz (Fulks & Foulkes), Fuson, deWitt, Depriest (de Priest), Harris, Hoskins, La Force, Le Fevers, Littell, Nantz (Nance), Napier, Parsons, Poteete, Pope, Maupin, Shakleford and Wildre are still found in the county. My grandmother had a brother named Steuben and I used to think they were calling him "Stewpang." When we dressed to go to a party, my father would ask if we were going to a "swaree" (soiree).

I believe the custom of giving the groom a "shivaree" was from French origin.

The Harris name is of French origin and Harrises are found in North Carolina and Virginia as early as 1750. Some of the other French families came to Mankantown, Va., and joined the Hugenot Colony. The first La Force was either Bene or Rene La Force and this family had to escape from France and become refugees.

One of the early La Fevers was an instructor at William and Mary College. The Maupin family joined the Hugenot Colony at Mankantown.

Henry Shackleford said in his application for pension that his name and that of his brother were on the mass roll when

PEOPLE, ANCESTRY, NEGROES, ETC.

he and his brother John were 16 years old. He was christened at Manken-Hick Church two miles from his father's in King William County, Va.

Manakin Colony was named for an Indian tribe.

It was customary to give the first man child the name of his father. People usually referred to the father as "old John Doe" and when he died John Doe was John Doe, Sr. Unless you can find a will or deed specifically mentioning his sons, it is hard to tell if the second John Doe is a junior or a nephew. Sometimes these names can be verified by Bible records, court records and graveyards.

Very often two cousins of nearly the same age would have the same name and then one would get a nickname such as "Slim John Doe" or "Little John Doe" or if the father of one was named James Doe, then his John became "Jim's John." Children called their parents mother and father, mama and papa, ma and pa, maw and paw, mammy and pappy, mum and pap, mod and pod. The grandparents were called practically the same except the "d" was not pronounced like "grammie and granpappy" or sometimes the grandchildren said "Big Mammy and Big Pappy."

When the Negroes were brought to Harlan County, they came as slaves and after emancipation day most of the old Negro families remained in Harlan County. One can still read their names like Brittains, Cornetts, Creeches, Crowleys, Greens, Herndons, Howards, Ledfords, Lewises, Renfros and Turners. Most of the owners were said to have been kind and considerate to them and many of the owners would not trade or sell them because they belonged to the family. My own granpaw had a chance to swap five slaves for a farm in the bluegrass but he would not part with them because they had been in his father's family. When I was a little girl, an old former slave named Uncle Jeff Green would come to visit us with my grandfather and I was eleven years old before I knew that he was not Granpaw's brother. He had some Indian blood and was a sort of leather color. After the war, when the Negroes were freed, they had no place to go and stayed at Granpaw Green's as long as he lived. He let them have a place to live and enough ground to raise what they needed and they got along about as they did before they were freed.

After the Civil War many of the Harlan County Negroes became freeholders of land but it is my understanding that Uncle Ransom Turner's property extended after death to his heirs. I was particularly fond of his wife Aunt Bets because she had been good to my mother whose mother had died young. Aunt Bets and her older sister Aunt Molly Turner used to help my grandmother when she was sick. The Turner girls were well trained by Mrs. William Turner who was a neighbor to my grandmother and she was beloved by both white and colored folks.

In 1888 the City colored school was located about where Watson's store is now. It sat back off the road about forty feet giving room for a playground. Most of the west side of the Main road was a field, called the "Big Field." The corner where Lee's Drugstore is, was vacant at that time but later John S. Bailey built a frame dwelling on that corner. A colored man by the name of Turner taught this school and he was related to Aunt Bets and Uncle Ransom Turner, who were well-to-do-landowners and a highly respected couple. Three of their children became schoolteachers.

Uncle Ransom Turner was a very large man—weighing around 300 pounds. When he rode into town on a big white horse he made a very imposing appearance. When I remember how he looked he must have been at least 70 years old and rode as well as a young man. However, when he pulled up to a hitching post, someone always offered to help him down from the horse but he usually made it by himself.

His wife, Aunt Bets, lived a long time after he died and in reminiscing, she said he was a handsome buck when he was young.

Uncle Ransom was quite dark but Aunt Bets was a light leather color. She said she was part Indian, and she certainly had some of the Indian features, especially high cheek bones.

She was a slave girl about the age of my grandmother and when quite young she was given in marriage to Uncle Ransom Turner. I recall Aunt Bets, who lived to be an old woman, very well, because she came to visit my mother once or twice a year. She had been a friend to my grandmother who was a neighbor to her family. All of Ivy Hill from

"Aunt" Elizabeth Turner, born 1845, widow of "Uncle" Ransom Turner. This picture was taken in 1932 by my cousin Grace Amanda Lewis, who walked up to their Lin Hollow home to take her picture. "Aunt" Bets was then almost 90 years old and had not seen Grace for 15 years. When she saw her, she turned to her granddaughters and said, "Why its Grace, John and Cora Lewis's girl."

where the city limits are now up to Lin Hollow was dotted with Negro cabins, and their graveyard was under a big tree which ground extended from the Harlan City School for about one block west and from Mound to Central Street.

When the war was over the family of Aunt Bets and Uncle Ransom settled in Lin Hollow, and it is my understanding that the William Turner family sold them the land at Lin Hollow for services rendered.

There was another old slave whom I recall named Uncle Press Turner and either his wife or sister used to help my grandmother (before I was born).

Aunt Bets and Uncle Ransom's children's ages corresponded with the ages of my mother and her sisters and brothers and when Aunt Bets' children married, then their children's ages corresponded with mine and my sisters. They married into Negro families who had settled here and many of their descendants live here now.

The Negroes were good storytellers and children always loved them because they were patient and told tales to children. Most of their tales turned to "hant" tales. They used to say that ghosts would gather at the graveyard and they could hear them singing under the big tree and one even said he had seen spooks gathered there. On Brittain Hill where there were many Negroes they said one end of the hill was hanted and they were afraid to go there because booghers came out after dark. The ghosts would roll kegs of fire right under your feet and you could not go past the ravine because hants of dead Indians held meetings and did not want folks around. They called this place Boogher Holler and it did look weird with forest trees covering this knoll. Lightning bugs would flit about in summer and occasionally an old log would send out an eerie phosphorus light and it is no wonder that it looked spooky. Even in daylight it looked dark and foreboding. Old-timers said that Brittain Hill was an Indian Burying Ground.

The Colored Grave Yard extended from about where the Trinity Episcopal Church is to the McDowell Home from Central to Mound Street.

Even as late as 1900, the native mountaineers spoke words and used expressions that were Chaucerian English or Shakespearean. Words like "pided" for spotted; fit for fought; ferninst, over against; scrouge or scrounge for crowded; behoof for behalf; holp or hope for help; joust for just; jounce for bounce; scroutch for crouch. To say you are clever means generous; if you are plagued, you are embarrassed; a chew was a chaw; a house of ill-repute a sporting house; a loose woman, a strumpet; a man who sought the attention of another's wife was a cuckold; to suckle was suck; to nuss was nurse; yaller was yellow; quare was queer; aeint was aunt; nary was not any; howdy was how-do-you-do; harry was how-

PEOPLE, ANCESTRY, NEGROES, ETC.

are-you; hallowbeye came before the telephone "hello." The accent was different; they put "y" in some words and "h" in others, like card pronounced cyard; carter-cyarter; garden-gyarden; here-hyear; there-thyear; heard-hyeurd; ear-year. It was hit, haint for aint; hease for ease.

Family names were pronounced like Creech was Scritch or Critch; Miracle was Marcle; Napier was Napper; Sergeant was Surgent; Parson-Passon, Hoskins-Hawskinses.

The customs were different. Most of the men wore a beard and the young man looked forward to growing a beard because it was the sign he had attained manhood and was considered honorable and commanded respect. They used the expression "to swear and affirm by the hair on their chin." They wore their hair quite long and when it was cut it was usually a home-job, sometimes without scissors although nearly everyone possessed a razor to trim hair.

Writing pens were cut from goose quills and quills were also whittled down for a toothpick and nearly every man would carry a quill pick in his pocket.

Little girls wore pantalettes or pantaloons and boys wore long drawers for underwear. Children wore linsey-woolsey jeans even as they do today but little girls had to don petti-skirts when they were ten years old. After a girl became that age it was considered indecent for her to ride a-straddle so she had to sit sideways on a horse.

Babies were dressed warmly in undergarments knitted from the finest yarns and a bunting blanket was knitted or woven out of soft yarn to wrap the baby in when taking him out of his warm bed. Most babies slept beside their parents in the same bed but sometimes cradles were used to keep the grownups from rolling over on baby and smothering him.

The women usually wore linsey-woolsey, although in later times silk and cotton were obtainable and desirable. All women wore voluminous aprons made of flaxen cloth and when going out to visit they put on an extra fine apron trimmed in handmade lace and cross-stitching. The expression "put on your best bib and tucker" was true of these women. These aprons, of course, saved a lot of washing be-

Sally Clark Eager, born 1810, Wythe Co., Va., died Harlan Co. 1905 widow of George Washington Eager. She told her children she remembered when her father, John Clark, walked all the way home from the Mexican border after the War of 1812. He was wearing a red uniform jacket and brought her mother a small bottle of wine done up in straw covering. After this picture was made she lost her glasses when their home burned and she regained her sight until she could read and thread a needle.

cause they kept the dress skirt from getting soiled. Women in those days wore some sort of cap, everyday caps which they slept in and better caps for company and a handmade bonnet for church and funerals. The caps were always made of white flax and some of them had a little ruffle on them very much like the dust cap or boudoir cap some of you may recall. Later when black thin materials were easier to get some caps were made of thin black material. Not many of these people had an outer cloak but for outside wear everyone had a hand knitted shawl in various degrees of weight. These shawls were large, about a yard and a half square, and served many purposes. Many of the shawls were knitted or woven out of the natural color wool because it was hard to dye the yarns although dyed yarns were used. The stockings were knitted and some of them were finished off at the top with dyed bright blues, reds and greens. I recall the girl that one of my uncles married said she came to the town of Mount Pleasant

PEOPLE, ANCESTRY, NEGROES, ETC.

to go to school and by this time in about 1890 the stores were carrying brought-on goods and the children in town were wearing coarsely knit factory milled cotton stockings. Her family lived across the Pine Mountain and her mother was knitting the wool stockings with the pretty red, blue and green tops (which by the way would sell for about $6.00 a pair in a sports-goods store now) and she longed for a pair of the brought-on store-black stockings.

Most of the settlers had large families and they gave the same names to their children that their parents or grandparents had had. Some of these names are not used very much now, such as: Aaron, Abel, Abner, Abijah, Absheer, Absolam, Abraham, Achilles, Adam, Addison, Adron, Adolphus, Aron, Albert, Aley, Alpha, Alonzo, Ambrose, Amon, Amos, Andrew, Alexander, Arthur, Augustus; Babat, Bascom, Basil, Berry, Bartholomew, Beriah, Bonapart, Boaz, Brutus, Boyd, Burl, Buford; Calvin, Caleb, Caesar, Carter, Cassius, Carlos, Cato, Chadwell, Christopher, Claiborne, Claud, Chester, Chauncey, Columbus, Cody, Cornelius, Crittenden; Daniel, David, Dillon, Dionishus;. Ebeneezer, Elza, Eli, Elijah, Elias, Emert, Elizha, Elkhanah, Elihu, Emmett, Enoch, Enos, Endow, Emil, Ephriam, Ezekial, Erasmus, Esaw, Ewell, Ezra, Ethan; Farris, Farmer, Felix, Fielding, Ferdinan, Fredrick, Floyd; Gabriel, Geoffry, Gideon, Granite, Gustavus; Herman, Harvey, Harrison, Hector, Heronimus, Hezekiah, Hiram, Hobart, Horace, Hoseah, Harmon, Hampton, Homer; Ike, Ira, Isaiah, Isaac, Isham, Israel; Jehu, Jerden, Jonah, Jonas, Jacob, Jason, Jackson, Jasper, Jepe, Jeremiah, Justus, Joel, Jesse, Jefferson, Jonathan, Josiah, Joshua, Josephus; Karl, King; Larkin, Lazarus, Lafayette, Lemuel, Lester, Leander, Levi, Leonard, Leopold, Laurance, Lloyd, Leroy, Luke, Luther; Marcellus, Marcus, Mark, Martin, Matthias, Matthew, Micajah, Milbourne, Milton, Malachi, Maximilus, Mordicai, Morgan, Moses, Murle, Mortimer, Morton; Nehemiah, Nathan, Nathaniel, Nimrod, Noah, Noble, Normas; Obadiah, Omega, Oliver, Orion, Orville, Oscar; Palonius, Pierre, Perry, Paschal, Pearl, Phebus, Phillip, Paris, Pressly, Proctor, Prophet; Quinton, Quillan; Radford, Roscoe, Randolph, Ralph, Ransom, Reuben, Reason, Rufus; Samuel, Sampson, Saint Clare, Sebastion, Selvester, Shadrack, Silas, Simon, Solomon, Spencer, Speed; Taursus, Taylor, Theophilus, Theodore, Titus, Timothy, Tobias, Tyrus; Uriah; Vaschal, Vernon, Vester, Valentine, Vincent, Victor, Virgil, Vivion; Walter, Washington, Warren, Wilkerson, Wilson, Wheeler, Wright; Xerxes; Yerkes, York; Zaccheus, Zachariah, Zebulon, Zed, Zion.

It is said that a couple could not agree on the name for their new baby, so they agreed to open the Bible, and whatever word the finger found, that would be the name of the baby, so they came to a passage, "Verily, verily, . . ." and the child was named Verily, which happened to be a girl.

Popular names for girls were: Abigal, Adah, Adeline, Alafair, Alabama, Alabaster, Almeda, Almira, Amanda, Amelia, America, Angelita, Areatha, Armilda, Arminta, Arabella, Artemis, Augusta; Barthenia, Belinda, Beatrice, Bertha, Blanche, Beulah; Cameo, Camelia, Cameliza, Calabash, Carlotta, Cassandra, Charity, Clarinda, Clarissa, China, Chloe, Comfort, Constance, Crystal, Christiana, Cumile, Cynthia; Delpha, Della, Delia, Delilah, Deborah, Diana, Delorah, Desdamona, Dinah, Dicie, Drucilla, Dulcina; Elleander, Easter, Emily, Esther, Estelle, Elnora, Elizah, Evaline, Emoline, Eulalah, Eunice, Euphemia, Euridice; Faith, Florida, Florence, Francine, Felicity; Geneva, Georgia, Gertrude, Gwendolyn; Hannah, Harriet, Henrietta, Hester, Heather, Hilda, Hibiscus, Hope, Honora; Imogene, Iris, Isabella, Irene; Jemima, Jerusha, Jacqueline, Juanita, Judah, Julia, Joicy; Latitia, Laura, Lavinia, Leah, Lela, Linda, Louisiana, Lucinda, Lucretia, Lula, Lydia; Mahalah, Malissa, Malinda, Matilda, Melany, Melody, Minerva, Marcia, Maxine, Maudelle; Naomi, Narcissus, Natalie, Nancy, Noriah, Norene, Nola; Obedience, Octavia, Olive, Orlena, Orpha, Ola, Oleander; Palestine, Patience, Patriot, Patricia, Penelope, Perlina, Phebe, Paulina, Pisca, Pleasant, Precious, Priscilla, Prudence; Rachel, Radiance, Rebecca, Rejina, Rosaline, Rosaman, Rozelle, Rozine; Savannah, Sabenia, Seretta, Serepta, Serena, Sophia, Sylvesta, Sylvania, Suzannah; Tabitha, Talilah, Temperance, Theodocia; Varilla, Verdenia, Vestenia, Victoria, Violet, Viola; Zella, Zenia, Zelphia, Zilpah, Zadah, Zelena, Zulema.

Very often a male child would be given an initial instead of a middle name like Harry "S" Truman. Again a child would be given three names like John Robert James Doe, and often the same name would be included in two sons' names like John Robert Doe and John Henry Doe.

Chapter X

RELIGION

WORSHIP of God in their own peculiar way caused many of our ancestors to settle in this country and the first thing they did was to pray, read or recite their Bible and Psalms and sing by heart their favorite religious songs. Very often the preacher was some hard-working man who led the service on the Sabbath. The first services were held in the homes but just as soon as enough neighbors got together, they wanted to build a house of worship. I am sure there were other early churches but the only one where we know of the location was on Tan Yard Hill by a branch named Meetin' House Branch because the log church they erected was called the Meetin' House. Like Abram in the wilderness it was their desire to build an altar to praise God. This log church was built on the land of Lewis Green and his wife Easter Kilgore Green (or Esther as it is sometimes spelled). A retired Revolutionary soldier with a crippled arm named James Hall testified in his application for pension that he lived two miles from Lewis Green, and it is practically certain that he preached at this Meetin' House. Lewis Green and his wife and several other graves were placed beside this church.

In a letter from Daniel Green, grandson of Lewis Green, Sr., son of Robert Green who married Comfort Howard, the second time, "My understanding was that grandfather built the church, I think about 200 feet from the river and just above the old road. I think about a half mile down river from Jack Parson's place. The Jack Parson's place was their home and he and his wife died there. There was a big sycamore tree that was leaning over the water directly south from the old church but suppose it is gone long ago. I cannot remember my father telling me anything of any preachers or contributors to the church. My grandfather was a very religious man and never allowed anything to interfere with his church attendance. I think no one of them has a tombstone;

RELIGION

they were marked with a slab as they did all graves practically at that time." This letter was written by Daniel Green when he was more than 70 years old in 1932.

I have been told that Lewis Green's father was a vestryman in the church at Kilgore Station in Virginia in Scott County before Lewis Green the Revolutionary soldier came to Harlan County.

In 1933 a regulation government tombstone was erected on this Revolutionary soldier's grave. In 1961 the new highway right-of-way was being constructed so these graves were moved to a location near another church a mile or so west and reinterred on property belonging to John Matt Pursiful.

Picture similiar in construction to the description of the log Meetin' House Branch Church, Tan Yard Hill.

This is beside a fenced-in private graveyard belonging to a Creech family.

The log Meeting House was described as a one-room log building with one door and a sod-clay floor, no window, and it is almost certain there was no fireplace or chimney. Papa, who was born in 1858, said he could recall that when they went to church in cold weather, stones were heated and

85

wrapped in cloths to keep their feet warm. He does not know whether the church they went to was the same old Meetin' House or another. The only ones who rode to church were the small children who were piled on a sled pulled by oxen team and the warmed stones were placed in the sled. When they got to the church they carried the stones in with them. In reading about some old churches in New England the writer said that their first churches had no heat and the preachers would take turns and this would go on for hours. The congregation would get so cold that they would clap their hands and stomp their feet to keep warm all the while the preacher was hollering above this noise.

There were no church services here in the summertime during the busy crop season and that left only a few days in the early spring and two or three months in the fall for church service to be held. On warm fall days the folks would walk barefoot to the church and stop when in sight of the church and put on their shoes. When a person died during the bad weather months the body was buried properly and then at a suitable time the funeral memorial was held. Sometimes as many as four or five funerals would be held together because there was either no one to preach the funeral or the weather was too bad to hold funeral services at the time of death. A bonfire was built outside the church at these preachings and the men would wander in and out of the church to warm by the fire and there was continual confusion going on during the preaching.

In the early days, it is not known what kind of baptism was used. We do know that some of the early settlers leaned toward the Church of England, the Hugenots, Lutherans, Quakers and other protesting denominations, but as time wore on the people seemed to prefer to dip the converts under the water in the river.

There is a story of a man who was converted at the old Meetin' House at Tan Yard Hill. He had, it seems, been a very wicked sinner so the day of his baptizing was set for a certain Sunday in the Cumberland River. He was a very large man, weighing over 300 pounds, so the preacher engaged four helpers to dip this man under and bring him to the top again. Word got around that there was to be this baptizing and people came from miles away, as far as the head of Poor Fork, Catron's Creek, and Yellow Creek to see "Big Bad John" go under. They expected the demons to wrestle and struggle to keep him from getting religion and they may have been a little disappointed when the baptizing progressed quietly and with dignity.

Baptizing in the Poor Fork River. Reverend Caleb Creech and Assistant. Jess Eversole, now over 80 years old.

The meeting house was used for other purposes besides preachings. Singing meets were held in the church when the singing master would strike a tuning fork which he carried with him and start singing; the others joined until they learned the words and the tune. A homemade fiddle, jew's-harp, or dulcimer was sometimes carried along to help out with the singing. When a schoolmaster got up a class they were allowed to use the meeting house to hold school.

The church services started early in the morning and continued until after a big basket dinner was spread outside if the weather permitted. They had to start home early in the afternoon so that they could get back in time to take care of the stock, chickens and milk the cows. We do not know for certain what the denomination of this Meetin' House was but we do know that they were religious, strict and preached "Hell and Damnation." The early denominations became Hard Shell Baptists and Shouting Methodists. About this time the Circuit Riders began to come through and the settlers were so proud and honored to have them visit in their home that they set out their best food and gave them their best bed. Usually a visitor had to sleep with some member of the family because rarely did they have a spare bed in those days.

Then there came the followers of Alexander Campbell and his church spread to the mountains. The first one that I recall was at Rosspoint on the bank of Poor Fork known as High Bank Church. At that time they were called Campbellites, but the name was not popular due to other people teasing them and asking to see the "hump of their backs." Later the name was changed to the Christian Church.

Before 1888 the United Presbyterian Church, referred to as Northern, sent missionaries into Harlan County to try to establish Sunday schools. They started a church in Harlan and built the first academy in Harlan County. The Presbyterian Church did not grow as rapidly as the other denominations because the people thought they were distant, cool and unfriendly. Actually they were dedicated to their work and sacrificed a great deal to come to the mountains.

RELIGION

The Presbyterian Church did not allow a man to preach unless he had a good education. In connection with the Harlan Academy there was a boarding home for the teachers and for students who lived too far away to attend day school. This school was operated on a paid tuition basis so the parents had to pay for sending their children to the academy.

The first Presbyterian minister was J. T. Reagan and the first services were held at the Masonic Hall in the old frame courthouse in 1886.

The Congregational Church came to Evarts in 1893 and established a church school which was known as the Black Mountain Academy. Professor E. Frank Dizney was the first principal (father of Howard Dizney who lives in town). The Dizneys with their five little Dizneys rode to Evarts in a jolt wagon drawn by mules. The first recorded preacher in Harlan County is James Hall, retired Revolutionary soldier. In his affidavit when he applied for disability in 1824, he stated that he "moved from Virginia into Harlan County which was then Knox where he resided 23 or 24 years and still resides, is known to every person in the surrounding country having been engaged for the last 14 years in trying to preach the gospel of Jesus." In another affidavit James Hall states that he is a clergyman residing in Harlan County, Ky., about two miles from William D. Green, residing in the same county and state and here certify that we are well acquainted with Lewis Green having known him for "20 year." In an affidavit of Elijah Green, J.P., he states that James Hall, "who has signed the foregoing certificate is a Clergyman to my own knowledge."

Among the early preachers in Harlan County were:
William Bailey—Methodist preacher born in Tennessee about 1860
Robert Bingham—Methodist preacher born about 1808
James Blevins—Baptist preacher born about 1821
Alfred S. Hall—Baptist preacher born about 1825
Andrew Miracle—Baptist preacher born about 1810
Solomon Pope—Methodist preacher born about 1812
Abner Turner—Christian preacher

Alexander Kelly—died at age 30 in 1858 at home of his father Jonathan Kelly, Jr., on Clover Fork
John Gilbert—Baptist preacher for sixty years, Revolutionary soldier who is buried in Clay County
Lewis Lyttle—Baptist preacher
George Spurlock—preached about 1840
George Brother—preacher in 1818
Noble Hall—preacher in 1870
W. Denham—preacher in 1856
Moses B. Evans—preacher in 1836
Rand Browning—Baptist preacher about 1870
Isaac Baker—Campbellite preacher. He was dramatic and preached that "Redmen of the forest reap the fat of the land before all nations."
Wiley Morris—Baptist preacher on Poor Fork
Henaphon Swinure—Methodist Episcopal Church South, performed marriage ceremony of George Washington Green to Maggie Ellen Rice, Jan. 10, 1888
J. Mahan—Baptist preacher
A. Shoemaker—Baptist preacher
Jonathan Day became a Presbyterian evangelist.

In the early days apparently there was not much of a line drawn between denominations because the people were so widely separated that all joined in one union. Later the denominations asserted themselves as more settlers arrived.

In the town of Mount Pleasant, Martha Creech Jones was the real founder of the Baptist Church. She moved from Hancock, Tenn., and married John Jones. Her father was a maker of hats and was known as "Hatter" Creech, though as far as I know they were not related to the Creeches who lived on Clover Fork, Poor Ford, and in the lower end of the county near Tan Yard Hill. She loved to entertain the visiting preachers and worked devoutly for the church. About 1872 she organized the first known Sunday school class for children. Years later Atty. John B. Carter was secretary for the class. The first Baptist Church building was on Central Street about where the McDowell Home is now and when Preacher Randolph Browning was the pastor, they lived

RELIGION

across in an old house which is still standing, though the church building is gone.

The oldest Methodist Church in town was the old Mount Pleasant Mission of the Methodist Episcopal Church, South. It was located between First and Second Streets and was later used for a schoolhouse. Apparently more of the Methodists who moved into Harlan County and referred to as "Northern" grew faster than the Southern Methodists so

PICTURE TAKEN about 1902
Judge Arthur B. Cornett holding his littlest girl Ella whose mother, Ella Amanda Hurst Cornett, died when she was born. Picture taken about 2 years after her death.
Other children, top row, Carrie; Denver; Ollie Cornett Lewis; Claude; bottom row, Ora seated in chair and Mary seated on ground.

sometime before 1890 the two churches merged. Old people recalled that it took several years to complete this union because the one church was submerged and lost in antiquity.

As far as I can learn the Methodist Episcopal Church built the first frame church on the site where the brick church now stands known as the "Ella Cornett Memorial."

The first Christian Church in town was built in the "Big Field," now Cumberland Avenue, and it was of frame construction. At that time they were known as Campbellites. This church was built after 1900 because the first one that I recall was about five miles north, northeast of Harlan on High Bank near Rosspoint, and known as the High Bank Church.

When Capt. Ben Harris' will was produced in court (Will Book, I p. 60), April 23, 1861, by his son, Thomas M. Harris, he left to his wife Sarah S. Burkhart Harris to hold her lifetime:

One comfortable house and good stone chimney, land, $50 ready money, 3 cows and calf, horse worth $75.00, plow, hoe and gearing, sidesaddle worth $22.00. $30.00 worth of hogs, all domestic fowls and the furniture. At her death he wanted all sold and 2/3 to go to treasurer of Methodist Episcopal Church, South, to be applied to foreign missions and residue put to interest to be paid annually to the Steward of the Mount Pleasant Mission, in addition to what "I have now given."

Except for the things he had already given to some of his children, his heirs were to share equally:

Thomas M. Harris	Betsy Crabtree
Alex Harris	Sarah Forester
Polly Bishop	John Harris
Rebecca Clark	Patsy Spurlock
Lavina Shumate	

Witness: Randolph Noe, James Browning
Executors, Solomon Pope and son Thomas M. Harris

Chapter XI

SCHOOLS

THE first schooling the pioneer children had was usually around the fireplace, provided someone could teach, had a slate and could read and write. This is one reason our written records are so meager. The slates had to be erased in order to write some other information. Any drawing which one might do in spare time was on a slate and erased for the next slate pencil. Paper was scarce, wrapping paper was not used here in the mountains during the earliest days and printed matter was scarce. The quill pen and ink writing was a laborious task for even the skilled scribe. As families multiplied the children were swapped around in the homes so that a member of one family could teach their children and the relatives' children for a few weeks usually referred to as "a spell" of time. The next few weeks they would alternate with all the children living with another family where one member could teach, thus giving the mothers time to do other things that were necessary in a household. Some of the pioneers could not read and write and often only one member in the family could teach.

A good bit of learning was done by the fireside. Bible verses were recited and learned by heart. A basketful of bright pebbles we called "jackrocks" were kept near the door and the children learned to count by adding or subtracting pebbles to their pile of rocks. Hymn singing and musical instruments were used around the fireplace and pickin' and singin' was enjoyed by all the family and some would pat their feet or clap their hands and learn what they could by listening. A family felt honored when they could have the schoolmaster as their paying guest because he was an addition to the fireside and usually kept on the good side of the men by helping at the barn and chopping wood. He usually made himself useful in other ways besides "larnin' " the "young-uns."

Spelling bees were something they looked forward to when they could have enough to choose sides and spell each other down. Some of the old folks were good spellers and pronounced words as they sounded because they learned to spell by syllables. For instance catastrophe was c-a-t cat, a-s catas, t-r-o catastro, p-h-e cat-as-tro-phe, catastrophe.

When the combined families' children became numerous, the pioneers felt the need of a schoolhouse where the children could be sent to learn to read and write and figure multiplication. The schoolhouse was a one-room log house with a chimney and fireplace which the schoolmaster had to build and refuel with the help of the pupils. The expense of the log schoolroom was borne by the families who wanted their children to learn the three R's. The house was built on private land which belonged to one of the families. The early schoolteacher was usually a man who collected tuition from the parents with anything the parents had to trade, for most of them had no silver with which to pay. In return the schoolmaster took turns staying with the different families, boarding and rooming with one family a few weeks and then boarding and rooming with another family. Later a Board of Trustees was formed and for many years schoolteaching was carried on in the same manner except that the Board of Trustees decided on the person they wanted as teacher.

These little schoolhouses were bare except for a few crude benches. The schoolmaster provided the slate and allowed the pupil to take his turn at using the slate. The schoolmaster's "larnin'" was usually his head as he rarely possessed a book. The schoolmaster was looked up to as a scholar and highly respected. Schoolteaching provided a start in life for a young fellow because what little he received in trade, goods, or other pay was considered clear profit. The early churches were used for schoolhouses which did not interfere with preaching.

These early schools were called subscription schools because the schoolmaster had to collect his own tuition from the parents. It was unusual for a woman to be a schoolteacher in the earliest day but women did teach in later years. My

SCHOOLS

own grandmother taught a school in 1875 which was unusual for a married woman. She had to be away from her home and husband except on weekends so she taught only one term.

Quite frequently the schoolmaster was also a singin' master and would hold singing meets either in the schoolhouse or meetinghouse. He was a great lion and had a tuning fork which he would strike for the pitch to start the song. He would begin to sing and those who knew the song would join in and others would learn "by heart" the words and the tune by practicing, until they learned to sing it from memory.

During the winter months the weather would be too bad for the children and the teacher to walk to the school so it was not practical to have school in the worst weather.

After the Civil War, the old log clerk's office was used for a schoolroom and when court was not in session the new frame courthouse was used for school, usually in the Masonic Hall which was upstairs. After the brick courthouse was built in 1888, the old frame courthouse was used for school and other meetings. John Ancil Ward, who was a fine scribe, taught school here as did many other schoolmasters.

My own father taught a subscription school in 1878 and earned $40.00 clear money which he used to start into the merchandise business. By that time a teacher could hope for the school year to last three to five months.

Some of the schoolmasters who taught in the frame courthouse were: Smith Hayes, Joe Ball, a Presbyterian preacher J. T. Reagan and a "little bitty" woman named Jenny Campbell. Miss Delora Osborne from West Virginia taught kindergarten for the Presbyterian school in this building before the academy was finished. Judge William Floyd Hall came here to teach in the same building. He wore a frockcoat trimmed in braid and when it became frayed, he went to my grandmother, Mrs. Henry Clay Rice, to have his coat mended. He later read law and became a legal barrister.

Other schoolteachers in the county were S. J. Critt Howard, Eli Huff and George Black. A fellow named Ely taught school in the old Mount Pleasant Southern Methodist Mission building which was across from the post office, between First and Second Streets. Cora Rice went to school here and Frankie Skidmore, who was a widow, went to school so that she could learn to teach.

Up until last year in 1961 there were two of the one-room schools left. Salt Trace school was abandoned by the Board of Education, and as of this year there was an unused one-room log schoolhouse left on Martin's Fork, but probably it is one of the passing landmarks.

One of the oldest schoolhouses in the county was on the property of John Lewis on Poor Fork River. Up until a few years ago it was still standing. Another very old schoolhouse

One-room log school house, Salt Trace

was built of logs on Catron's Creek which was known as Beech Grove. It was built halfway between two farms owned by the Carters and Eagers who were brothers-in-law so that their children could go to school. There is an old cemetery nearby and probably preaching was held in the schoolhouse. Before the Carters and Eagers built this schoolhouse the mothers, who were sisters, took turns teaching each other's

SCHOOLS

children. One mother would keep all of the children one month, sewing, baking, teaching and caring for them and the next month the other mother would take her turn so the children could learn what they could teach them.

Contrary to the impression many people have of the old settlers, many of them could write or sign their names. In looking over transactions on the old record books, some of them made their "x" instead of signing their name. I have never practiced writing with a quill pen, but you must understand that these old folks worked with their hands, and often the knuckles became enlarged and stiff with rheumatism, wind, weather and calluses. It is understandable that when they came to the point of signing their names, it was simpler and easier to let the clerk, who was used to it, write their name and then they touched the pen.

Usually the women's hands were not so rough even though they worked hard and often made the garden and hoed in the cornfield; they also cooked and knitted and did the spinning and sewing for the family. Handling grease and tallow kept their hands softer and the needlework kept the fingers more supple than the men's hands. However, women had very little time to practice writing with a quill so they often touched the pen for their signature when actually they were literate enough to write on a slate. Many of the old-timers would read but it was their custom to recite, quote and spell orally. Messages were sent by word of mouth and a man would go two miles out of his way to deliver a message, and I mean it would be almost verbatim.

Old Judge W. C. L. Huff born in 1846 on Poor Ford, moved to Harlan and attended school where his brother Eli Huff taught at the Beech Grove School and boarded at "old man Carter's."

Some of the old people sent their children to other places to learn to read, write, spell and "figger," and they would come back and teach others in turn. My own father was sent to the Baptist Institute at Barbourville, Ky., in 1875 and then he came back to teach.

Many of the pioneers could trace their name even though they could not read or write.

The Blue Back Speller is the most familiar old book which was used by the schoolmasters. Later the McGuffey Reader was the standard book. After blackboards came into use the schoolteacher wrote the words or sentence on the board and the children practiced trying to get that flowing perfection. Most of the children could provide a slate pencil because it could be whittled out of some kinds of rock.

About 1886 the Presbyterian Church sent missionaries into the county to establish a school. First they held Sunday schools and then followed the academy, church and a boarding home for the teachers and students. The Presbyterian Academy was built in 1888 and was used up until about 1910 when the graded school was built. They also established a school and church at Smith, Ky.

The Congregational Church established a school at Evarts in 1893 called the Black Mountain Academy. Professor E. Frank Dizney (father of Howard Dizney) who had taught in the Presbyterian Academy became the Principal of the Black Mountain Academy. At one time it served about 240 pupils and was used up until about 1917.

In 1897 a Miss Pettit and a Miss Miller came in to Harlan County, looking for a place to locate a nondenominational school in the mountains. They walked over many parts of the county looking for a site where the needs would be served. One day they were in the Pine Mountain area and during the day, they became tired and thirsty and sat down to rest. On their way, someone had given them a gourd and they saw a cow standing under a tree nearby, so they decided to get a gourd full of milk. While they were trying to get the cow to stand still, along came a farmer who offered to milk for them. He milked a gourd full for each of them and they thanked him and wondered who owned the cow and the farmer answered "I do."

These two ladies went farther into the mountains and when it came time to look for a place to spend the night they came upon a small log cabin and asked if they could

Courtesy the Pine Mountain Settlement School

William Creech and Sallie Dixon were married in 1866. Picture taken when they celebrated their golden wedding. Her father sent to the settlements at Lexington, Ky., for her dress pattern. It was probably jaconet, a fine linen-lawn like material popular at that time. It was made with fine hand work and loving care went into the fashioning of this treasured wedding dress, which she wore again on their fiftieth anniversary.

spend the night. An old couple were living there and told them they would be welcome. The house was small but clean and Miss Pettit was amazed to see real flaxen sheets on the spare bed which were trimmed with handmade lace. They were delighted with the old coverlid and the homespun appearance of the place and impressed with the genteel hospitality of the couple.

Later on Miss Pettit was intrumental in establishing the Pine Mountain Settlement School where Mr. William Creech donated the land.

CHAPTER XII

CUSTOMS

THE old courtship customs differed entirely from our modern ways. The pioneer girl certainly had the advantage of today's girl because men outnumbered women. The qualities that attracted a man then were somewhat different. The old-fashioned male looked for a good housekeeper, one who was not afraid of work and a healthy girl who could present her lord and master with many sons and daughters in order to keep up the work of a big farm. A robust, portly lass with a buxom shape ranked higher than the slender, frail-looking girl. My father used to compliment a woman when he said she was a fine, portly woman.

"Uncle" John Shell born about 1814. When he died at the age of 108 in 1922, a Lexington, Ky., paper, headlined him as the oldest man in the world. When he was 105 years old, he was a guest of the Governor at the Kentucky State Fair in Louisville, Ky.

CUSTOMS

Some swains asked permission of the girl's parents to "keep company" but more often they "took to going together" with the parents' permission and they generally understood that he was "sparkin' the gal." If a mountain youth seemed shiftless and lazy the parents often opposed the match. Most of the courting was done with the parents' consent. When calling on a girl the suitor would spend the night in the home of the parents on account of living too far apart for him to make a trip to see the girl and then return to his home in one day.

Both the young girls and young men were so bashful it is a wonder they ever understood each other. When it was time to eat dinner the girl was too timid to sit at the table and she would wait until the men folks left the table before she would sit down to eat. The suitor was expected to get up from the table when the host did and accompany him on his round of chores, helping with the feeding and even milking the cows.

When they went to a "meetin' house" the whole family went along with them. The women folks usually sat together at one side of the church and the men folks at the other side.

If there was a dance in the community the whole family attended and the girl went along with her family and the boy went with his. They would return to their homes the same way although everyone knew they "were keepin' company."

It was necessary to get a license to marry and if a preacher was not available then the Justices of the Peace, called "Squires," were vested with authority to perform marriages. The marriage record was sent to the county seat together with a marriage bond, which bond needed to be signed by the girl's parents if she were under the legal age. Two witnesses' names were written on the application for license. The man who officiated at the wedding usually took the license to the county seat for record. It was a long trip to the county seat so the parson or "squire" would wait until he had several before he took them to be recorded. The participants of the wedding were referred to as the "weddiners."

Very often the couple's first child was born before the

marriage was ever recorded. Every family kept Bible records and someone in the family was very particular to "set down" the dates of the marriages, births and deaths in the family.

The weddings were something to celebrate when the whole countryside joined in to make it a festive occasion. The bride's trousseau was scant by today's standards, but the parents furnished her with a dowry which consisted of spare feather beds, feather ticking, pots, pans, home-woven blankets, coverlids, linens and wooden utensils. A girl was not given land as were the boys probably due to a throwback of the old feudal system when the male heirs occupied the land. The wedding usually took place at the bride's home where they spent the first night and then the groom took her to the groom's home where a feast was prepared called the "infare or infair."

The custom of shivareeing the groom was carried on by some of their friends and sometimes these friends became too enthusiastic, just as fraternity initiations are today. Often the bridegroom would be carried off bodily and kept away from the festivities for hours and in their zeal, they would ride the groom on a rail. This custom kept up in this county until about the time of World War I and rice-throwing was substituted, together with tin cans and old shoes being tied on the going-away car.

The infare was prepared at the home of the groom. Everyone attended who possibly could. My mother told about going to a wedding here in town with her sister when they were small girls about eight or ten years old. George Brittain Turner's daughter, Louise Turner, was marrying a man named Milton Jones, at the bride's home which was situated where the Anderson-Laws Funeral Home now is. The wedding was held in the yard and the bride was dressed all in white with a wreath in her hair. Her dress material was imported and was called jaconet, which was a sort of linenlike lawn material. This took place about 1884 at the old home place which was a big two-story log house. The big summer kitchen also built of logs was a few feet from the main house and here the wedding feast was prepared by former Negro

CUSTOMS

slaves of the Turner family. Uncle Press Turner was the boss cook and they had ham, turkey, chicken, and every kind of vegetable on hand with several kinds of cake, served with egg custard. Ice cream was not made at that time although a few people built ice-houses on the river bank, filled them with sawdust and could keep ice sometimes as late as July. Ice was usually reserved for the care of the sick. My mother, sister and the other smaller children were excited because they had never before seen anyone dressed in all white.

There was a smaller log house at the back of the house which had been used for slave quarters but now kept furnished for extra guests so the little log house was fixed up for the honeymoon night. The small children peeped in after the bride and groom went to their little house and saw them embracing.

The next day the groom took his bride to his father's home where another feast was prepared. The home place is at the west end of Harlan where their son, Dr. J. B. Jones, lives now. Mrs. Jones was widowed and is now Mrs. Gilbert and living at 96 in 1962.

My aunt, Cora Rice, married John Blanton Lewis at her grandfather Rice's in Tazewell, because her mother was dead. The parents of the groom lived at Four Mile Farm (now owned by Bryan Whitfield II), and they prepared the infare for the bride and groom. At that time the Southern Railroad was building a road from Knoxville to Middlesboro about 1894 and had to tunnel through the mountain at Cumberland Gap. The road was blocked and the John B. Lewises arrived two days late for the infare at the Felix Goldwin Lewis Farm.

Everyone looked forward to a couple producing an heir and if a child was not born within a year or two the whole countryside was disappointed because a prolific couple would raise from twelve to fifteen children. If the firstborn was not a boy there was a little disappointment and very often the girl was given the name of a man-child or her father's name. The baby girl though proved more comfort and help to the mother as she learned to do chores around the house.

When a child was born it was the time of great rejoicing because both the girl's and the boy's parents hoped to have descendants. Alliances with some families meant great strength and prestige and usually the more descendants the more could be accomplished. The birth itself was a simple affair which was taken as a matter of natural course and often the child was born without benefit of a doctor. The pioneer was careful to "set down" the name and date of the child's birth in the Bible and many times this was the only written record of the child's birth. It was customary to give the child a name to honor one or both sides of the family and family names were carried on for generations.

Death was considered an act of God and was accepted with somber solemnity. If there was a preacher in the community and weather permitted a funeral was preached immediately. But if weather was bad the body was given a decent burial and memorial services were preached several months later when the weather was good. Most all the graveyards were a few hundred feet from the home place where a stone slab was erected and the name, date of birth and death were crudely scratched on it with a piece of metal or nail. Time and weather have obliterated nearly all the old markers so that many are illegible. However, at the time of the burial and the lifetime of two or three generations everyone knew who was buried in which place. As grandchildren moved away or the land passed into other hands many of the graves are unknown today.

After death the body was prepared by friends and neighbors and they made sure by every known test that life had departed with the spirit. The body was washed and lotions rubbed over the features to retard as much mortification as possible. The eyes were closed and the lids weighted with coins and sometimes a bandage had to be tied around the head and jaws to keep the mouth closed. Every household kept back suitable cloth to make a shroud and line the coffin. Some people prepared their own dress. The heads of the women were covered with white caps and some women made special caps to "be laid away in." Very often the man had already selected a suitable slab for the tombstone.

In the meantime the women had prepared food in large quantities because neighbors and relatives remained at the home and a group of men always "set up" all night with the corpse. The men prepared a coffin and the women lined it with cloth and the body was ready for the funeral. If no preacher was available some friend read or recited passages of scripture and prayed and recited psalms. The coffin lid was pegged down with wooden pegs and carried to the grave which had been dug by friends and neighbors. They usually selected a knoll on a hillside for a graveyard and the coffin was placed with the head toward the east. After the coffin was lowered by strong men into the grave friends and neighbors began dropping clods of clay sod. Did you ever hear the sound of doleful clods falling with a hollow echo on the wooden coffin? Believe me! No sound has ever been reproduced like it on the stage, screen, radio or television. All graveyards were near the home place in the family property or a nearby meetin' house. When the swollen streams and winter weather prevented a funeral from being recited to their satisfaction, then memorial services were held months after the death.

There have been stories of paid mourners and wailers but personally all the funerals that I have attended have had enough relatives and friends to mourn that it certainly was not necessary to pay anyone to come in and act. Once I heard a mother shout out loud, "Glory to God! God's will be done," during her young son's funeral, and to me that seems sweet because we are taught that we are to be submissive to God's will. These memorial services almost a year after the death of a loved one were pure torture but the people accepted them as was customary. These memorial services lasted for hours, in fact more than one dead person may have funerals preached at the same time. Sometimes these services were preached at the graveyard and again they would be preached at the meetinghouses, depending on the families involved. All the women prepared big baskets of food to take to the services and the meeting had to be recessed while everyone ate food from a well-spread board. All the scraps of food were placed back into the basket to take home to the chickens and hogs, for no food was ever wasted.

When the funeral services were held at the graveyard, usually the grave headstone had not been placed and it was placed at this time. Everyone knew where everyone was buried so some of the slabs never were marked. This is not so simple now when trying to locate a grave unless you can locate an old person who attended one of the funerals and was told where certain bodies were buried. Even then they described a place as being marked by a hickory tree, small holly or some variety of tree and by the time another generation is looking for a grave marker, the tree has grown beyond the old description or another taken its place.

Graveyards were important to the pioneer and when locating the grave of an old Revolutionary soldier named Stephen Jones, a group of men carried an old man on a sick litter for miles up a rocky creek (I think the name was Jones Creek) so that this old man who was a descendant of the

On this peak rests Stephen Jones; like Abram in the Wilderness his remains were undisturbed and in 1940 a Government Tombstone was erected for his service in the Revolutionary War.

CUSTOMS

Stephen Jones could show where the Revolutionary soldier was buried.

My great-grandfather, George Washington Eager, lived on Catron's Creek about three and one half miles from Mount Pleasant and when he died about 1883 the river was swollen and past fording. Four of his neighbors came into town to have a coffin made and they carried the coffin all the way and walked except where they had to cross the Cumberland River at the south end of Mount Pleasant someone "set them across the river" by paddling a boat. His widow lived to be 94 years old and I have often wished that I could have been old enough to understand her stories. At the time she died in 1905 I was a small girl of seven but my aunts and uncles remembered and related many of the tales my great-grandmother told them.

About 1882, my mother, her sister and Aunt Sade Turner Creech, a Negro, once walked all the way to Farmer's Mill which was about five miles from Mount Pleasant, to a funeral. This was a memorial service to be held at the meetinghouse nearby where the family lived. This was a postponed funeral because the person had died in the winter and many people gathered in respect for the family. These girls carried their shoes and walked barefoot all the way until they came within sight of the meetinghouse. There they stopped at a branch to wash their feet and put on their shoes.

When some member of the family was absent at the time of death the person would have been buried before the member of the family returned. I was not old enough to remember when friends of my parents had a child who became ill while his father John Ancil Ward was on a selling trip through the mountains. He was a drummer and took his samples in a buckboard which was about the only kind of conveyance that would stand up under our roads except the jolt wagon and sled. This child who was a little older than I was was buried two weeks before Mr. Ward could get home.

My grandfather, Henry Clay Rice, and his brother, John Robert Rice, married sisters, daughters of George Washington Eager, Sr. John Robert Rice's wife died at their home in Pineville, and about that time there came a flood and the rivers got so high that people could not cross the streams. My uncle wrote to his brother who lived in Harlan and said, "Henry, by the time you receive this letter, my wife Serepta will be underground."

My grandmother Rice died rather young and it was not suitable to hold the funeral at that time, so some months later a memorial service was held in the Masonic Hall of the old courthouse which was opposite the Rice home. In the meantime, my grandfather had married a lady named Elizabeth Smith, and she sat beside him at the funeral, herself expecting, holding the dead woman's baby boy on her lap, grandpaw holding the littlest girl and my mother and her sisters and brothers were strung along the pew, listening to the preacher memorialize the death of his first wife and the mother of the children.

This second wife Elizabeth died giving birth to her first child, and my grandfather married the third time, this time to a girl as young as my mother, named Elizabeth Neal.

Certain standards of behavior were customary for a widow. She must stay at her own home for a period of several months although she could visit her parents or her dead husband's parents. A heavy black veil was worn to cover her head called a widow's bonnet and her dress must be somber; otherwise the neighbors would criticize her. If she stayed at home and worked at the house and attended to the farm business then she was above reproach. After this period of mourning was over then the widow was "settin' out" and was eligible for courting. The men outnumbered women in those days so it was more unusual for a woman to remain a widow than it was for her to remarry. The widower's standard was not as strict as the widow's because a man did not get "talked about" but a widow's reputation could be easily damaged.

Many families became involved in feuds which were usually caused by two friends and relatives "falling out" over something. These grievances drew in other members of the family and these feuds often lasted for years. One feud which lasted through two generations spilled over into this county because some members of the families moved in order to avoid becoming involved in their differences.

Another feud originated within our own borders and caused many other families concern besides the immediate relatives. It was hard for their friends and neighbors to remain neutral. This feud occurred before I was born but I have heard people say that tension became so strong that at one time the State Militia was called into the county to keep down trouble. This Militia unit marched into Harlan County and during their march they had to make camp. While around the campfire one of the men accidentally discharged his gun while cleaning it. Wild rumors spread from one town to the other and in a week or so reporters were sent into the county to write up the story of the Harlan Battle.

Christmastime was a happy celebration and any or all of the children who were away from their parents either came to spend the Christmastime with one or the other parents. The very best feast possible was prepared with whatever meats were at hand, vegetables that had been saved up for Christmas, dried stewed fruit and punkin butter (pumpkin), coffee, molasses, cider and gingerbread for the children. The mother provided knitted stockings for the children to hang by the fireside and whatever gifts they could get were placed in the stockings. Perhaps some nuts, apples, and a stuffed doll and whittled wood toy for the boy comprised Santa's gifts. Handmade presents were given to all the family such as knitted mittens, caps, gloves and the like. They decorated a little with strings of popcorn and strings of red berries but there was not much room in those houses then to decorate. Sometime during Christmas the man of the house recited or read the Christmas story from the Bible and they repeated the Lord's Prayer together.

CHAPTER XIII

ARTS, MUSIC, POETRY

THE early settlers were poetical minded; they loved the Psalms and learned many by heart. Their natures responded to the liquid notes poured out by the shepherd boy in the Psalms. Some of them could recite whole chapters of the Bible and many of the passages expressed their feelings when the majesty of the mountains wove its spell. The Bible was usually the only book possessed by these early people although some of them knew a little of Shakespeare's stories from hearing them recited. Most of their learning was an oral matter and not of their own reading. Some of these people had an almanac which they read and reread until its pages were dog-eared. They learned a lot from the almanac, besides the weather, because it would give information on many subjects which interested them very much.

Music, singing and dancing were enjoyed by the early pioneers. Some of the old mountain dances were the hoedown, the buckwing and the jig. The Virginia Reel and square dance were also popular and later came the minuet and schottish which were too tame for the rugged folk.

The Pine Mountain Settlement School revived some of the native dances and when Director Glynn Morris was there he trained a troup which went on tour. The dancers went through their sets with such precision that they were invited to dance at the White House before President and Mrs. F. D. Roosevelt. One of their dances was a sword dance which they did to perfection. Another dance was the Kentucky Running Step and after hearing about this dance a man from England went to visit Pine Mountain Settlement School to observe this dance. Information was that he was a former tutor of the Prince of Wales and his hobby was old country dances. He identified this dance as one that had been lost in England for more than a century, but it had been kept alive here in the Kentucky mountains and was called simply the Kentucky Running Step. It had been brought over from England when some of their ancestors had come to America and settled here in the mountains.

The handiest music was whistling or singing, and the easiest instruments to carry about were the tuning fork and the mouth harp or harmonica. Someone in a family practiced until he could play a tune. Then the men began to make fiddles and dulcimers and although they were crude, the instruments were used. Later the hand organ, the melodeon and old square piano came into this section.

The whole family participated in the dances which were either square dances or the Virginia Reel. Sometimes they gathered in the homes where there was enough room or the schoolhouse to hold these dances. A fiddler and a caller were absolutely essential to a dance and some of them were good. The fiddler was helped by singers and the fiddler knew his tunes "by heart." One of the old favorites was "Turkey in the Straw" and while he was playing others would clap to the rhythm and others sing as they went through their sets. The caller in his big booming voice would call off the sets to keep the dancers moving—"dress your pardner," "hands right," "doshie doe," "to your places," "salute your pardner." The dancers responded with perfect timing because they knew the routine and indeed a stranger would not be able to understand the words the caller said as he called them out in a singsong voice with amazing rapidity. As the evening wore on and the singers waxed eloquent they added verses to the songs making up lines as they sang.

There were "Duck Foot Sue," "Shortenin' Bread," "Polly Put the Kettle On," "Skip to My Lou" and "Yankee Doodle Dandy," but probably the most popular was "Sourwood Mountain":

"My hound dog can tree a coon cat, Hey-diddle-diddle de day
Barks to tell me where he's at, Hey-diddle-diddle de day

I guess I'm just a mountain bounder, Hey-diddle-diddle de day

I've been somewhat a rounder, Hey-diddle-diddle de day

But git me a gal that won't founder, Hey-diddle-diddle de day
I'll show ye a man who won't wonder (wander), Hey-diddle-diddle de day

My gal lives on Sourwood Mountain, Hey-diddle-diddle de day
She won't see me cause she's poutin', Hey-diddle-diddle de day

She lives way over in Letcher, Hey-diddle-diddle de day
She won't come and I won't fetcher, Hey-diddle-diddle de day

She's as pretty as a daisy, Hey-diddle-diddle de day
She's not slow, she's not lazy, Hey-diddle-diddle de day

She lives in the head of the holler, Hey-diddle-diddle de day
She won't come and I won't call her, Hey-diddle-diddle de day

I went on to see her anyhow, Hey-diddle-diddle de day
She was helping her paw to plow, Hey-diddle-diddle de day

I pitched in and milked the cow, Hey-diddle-diddle de day
Then they made me swill the sow, Hey-diddle-diddle de day

Then I got tired of totin', Hey-diddle-diddle de day
This is the end of my courtin', Hey-diddle-diddle de day

Then there was "Polly Wolly Doodle" which verses could be improvised and added to and some of the familiar lines are

ARTS, MUSIC, POETRY

"I went to bed but it wasn't no use, Sing Polly Wolly Doodle all the day
My feet stuck out for a chicken roost, Sing Polly Wolly Doodle all the day."

In later years old song became the favorites, such as "Lizie Jane," "Nellie Gray," "Old Black Joe," "Lost Chord," "Mocking Bird," "When You and I Were Young, Maggie," "After the Ball," "Suwanee River," "Lillie Dale," "Mid Camp Fires Burning—Blue Bell."
This poem was unsigned and unknown:

"Legends, poetry, music and thrills,
pour from trees, rocks, creeks and rills,
each primitive wind and storm, it stills
lifts to perch on Heaven's windowsills
Love-bound spirit, the corners it fills
cradles our lives in these dear old hills
as surely as the wheels of the old grist mills,
eternally chains our hearts and wills."

Biographic Quickie

"A-bornin', a-growin', a-singin', a-courtin', a-weddin', a-churchin', a-plowin', a-ailin', a-diein', a-buryin'."

CHAPTER XIV

INDIANS

THE early scouts who came through the county did not leave any written account but from legend it is thought that others came about the time Dr. Thomas Walker went through Cumberland Gap. These men followed the paths made by Indians who followed wild game to their watering places. It is said that some of the Indians were friendly and liked to trade with the white man. The Indians often paid off in gold which led the early white men to think there was gold in "them thar hills." Later the white men decided that the Indians had traded with other tribes in the Mississippi Basin and obtained the gold in trade. It is said that the Indian would give all his gold for one iron pot.

There were Cherokee Indians, remnants of some other tribe, perhaps the Shawnee, and the Quadrule. The Cherokee made their home in Virginia near Bristol and made excursions into Harlan, sometimes friendly, sometimes unfriendly. The Quadrules were said to have occupied Wallins Ridge and some of the tribes lived there permanently.

It is known that Indians were in Harlan County before the white man came and the last record of an Indian living here was a man named Sam Whitson. Although I do not recall ever having seen him, he did come into the town to buy a little tobacco, sugar and coffee. He lived on Clover Fork and people used to tease children and tell them the Indian would get after them when actually there was no harm in the old fellow. Elmon Middleton wrote a pamphlet on Harlan in 1934 and in it he said, "There is now an old Cherokee Indian who goes by the name of Sam Whitson, whom people sometimes see coming from his little hut near the top of Black Mountain at Coxton. He still wears his coal black hair in long plaited braids, dangling down his back."

Elmon Middleton describes the Quadrules in his pamphlet: "The Quadrules inhabited Wallins Creek and the

INDIANS

Cherokees were scattered in smaller bands throughout the County, some of them also living at Wallins Creek. The Cherokees usually were unfriendly and lived more secluded from the Whites. The Quadrules were very adept at spinning and weaving woolens and flax, making beautiful pottery. S. J. C. Howard, who died in Harlan just a few years ago, and who was formerly County Attorney of Harlan, gave many interesting accounts of this Colony of Quadrule Indians at Wallins. When a boy he used to hunt and fish with these Quadrule Indians at Wallins. They lived as a tribe at Wallins Creek until after the Civil War. . . . It is said that the Quadrule Indian girls were very beautiful. . . . Some married white people and today there can be found in Harlan County a few people who boast that they have Indian blood in them."

The Indians used many herbs for medicinal purposes and they told the white man where to look for roots, barks, leaves and plants which were right for certain cures.

The Indians were poetical and the names they gave to streams, trees and places are very musical. A few miles above Pineville is a place named Wasioto, so called by the Indians, meaning "Beautiful Banks of the Winding River." In the southern end of the county there was a deer lick or watering place which is now called Crummies Creek. The Indians called it the "Place Where Water the Great Deer Herd with the Crumpled Horns."

The old pioneers entertained their children with tales of Indian encounters which people had in earlier days. There was a fabulous Indian Cherokee Chief named Benge, also called Bange and Bench, who harassed the white people, particularly those who lived on the southern border of Virginia. Chief Benge and his band made their headquarters near Big Stone Gap. Va., and made excursions into Harlan County. James Green, brother of Lewis Green who settled in Harlan County, was killed by an Indian Chief Tassel, who was a brother or nephew of Chief Benge. James Green born 1757, died 1783.

There was a Captain Vincen Hobbs who lived on Catron's

Creek at the place now known as the Henry Smith Farm. This Captain Hobbs is given credit for killing Chief Benge. It seems that the State of Virginia presented Capt. Hobbs with a fine rifle for ridding the country of this warring chief. A rifle was just about the greatest trophy a man could have in those days. The early scout named Wallins is the first known white man who was killed by Indians. Turn to chapter six for this account.

In a copy of some Revolutionary soldiers a James Fraley, Floyd Co., Ky., in his application that "March 1, 1781, he again enlisted for nine months in Washington County, Va. to spy that season under Colonel Smith and Capt. Cowan. His range was changed. He and Samuel Auxier spied together that nine months on the headwaters of the Cumberland and Kentucky Rivers. The Shawnees camp up there the most frequent. A portion of the country he spied in is now Perry County and Harlan County, Ky. It was all Virginia then. This year, the Shawnees did more injury than any other year since 1775 or 1776. . . . In May, 1782 he spied in that section of the country altogether on the Clinch River, consequently altogether in Virginia, or the settlements here attached and the Indians killed Thomas Osbourne and Minny, his wife. He states that he helped bury them in the same coffin. They took two girls, Lucretia Osbourne, niece of Thomas Osbourne and Betsey Wall, prisoners to Canada and kept Lucretia Osbourne for four years. The Indians killed Betsey Wall by beating her on the head, he learned. Lucretia was exchanged and brought to Detroit where she remained till she married a man named Armstrong, who brought her back to Virginia and from whom she learned the fate of Betsey Wall. About that time they killed Mary Hamlin, wife of Henry Hamlin, and Isaac Newland. He states he is the identical man who killed the celebrated plunderer and Indian Chief, Bench." Please refer to top of page where our storytellers give Captain Hobbs credit for killing Benge and claim that he was presented with a rifle. Perhaps these two scouts were in the same posse.

INDIANS

There were at least three Indian Mounds in this county according to old-timers; one was named Brittain Hill where the Brittain home place was, another was at Wallins Creek and the other in the town of Mount Pleasant. Many Indian relics have been dug from this mound in Harlan because it is the site of the second courthouse and later there was more excavating and more relics found. From the bones found in this excavation it seems that there was a very large type of man with huge bones and skull and the other bones were of a smaller race. Some of them were in a sitting position.

It seems that some of the Indians played childish pranks which were nevertheless annoying and it is not known if they were watching the habits of the people for future attacks or whether they were unfriendly. The Indians knew where the white men got their water and when the spring was located far from the house, they would go to it and drink the milk and what they could not drink they would pour into the water and throw the butter on the rocks so the rocks would be slippery. When the family were all out in the fields working the crops, they would steal into the house and carry the yarn up into the loft or eat the food the housewife had ready for the next meal. Apparently these raids could have been murderous had the Indians been of a mind to kill at that time.

They tell the story about old Samuel Hoard, who came into this county about 1792. His son went to the spring and was just about to kneel down to drink when he caught sight of an Indian hiding behind a log. He ran as fast as he could to his home and his father took a gun to search for the Indian. In his haste the lad had left his hat on the log and they found no sign of the Indian but the hat was gone.

There is an old story about a woman being scalped by an Indian when she was a little girl. I have heard more than one version of the story but the gist of it is the same and I believe it to be true because the old people who told me were reared in different parts of the county and the story was told to them by their parents or grandparents. One version of the story was told to me by Mrs. Mose Howard who was Nancy Turner before her marriage and she was born in 1855. Her grandmother used to tell her stories and they lived near the people whose child was scalped. Then I have heard the story from "Uncle" Albert Ball who was a respected citizen who lived to be more than ninety years old and I have also heard it from Mrs. Felix G. Lewis who was Mary Blanton and was reared at Wallins Creek and also from Samuel Howard who was a grandson of the Revolutionary soldier Samuel Howard.

The Noes lived on Trace Gap, Burgoyne Branch, Coon Creek and Catron's Creek. They lived in a log house with a loft which served as a second story. This loft was easily accessible to an agile Indian from the outside of the house. The Indians would sneak into the loft and watch their opportunity to play tricks on the family. They were so quiet that no one knew they were around because the Indian was trained to walk like a cat from the time he could toddle. When Mrs. Noe would leave her weaving or spinning wheel to attend other chores, the Indians would cut her threads of wool and when she returned to her weaving she would spank her children when she discovered the mischief, thinking they were the culprits. Finally one day, the Indians who were always on the watch saw her husband leave and they knew that he was packed for a trip into the woods so they killed Mrs. Noe, tomahawked all the children and set fire to the home. One little girl four years old crawled out of the burning mass and crept to a spot in a cornfield close by. There she remained for two or three days subsisting on fresh corn and hiding all the time. White settlers who came to the scene found tracks around the house and knew that there were survivors and they would call out but no answer. The little girl thought it was the Indians again and was afraid. At last the settlers found her and took care of her. She lived to marry and rear a family of her own but it is said that she carried the horrible scar to her grave. Some folks said her scalp never entirely healed. Others said that she never went without a bonnet to cover her head. However, it was the custom for women to wear caps in the house so that is not unusual. This is not far from the place now known as Pansy. She married

INDIANS

William Irvine and according to birth records of Harlan County which were recorded at Frankfort during the period of 1852 to 1862 there were three children born to them as follows:
"Martha born 1853. Maiden name of mother, Noe. Father Wm. Irvine
Easter born 1859. Maiden name of mother, Fanny Noe. Father William Irvine
Nancy born 1861. Maiden name of mother Noe. Father William Irvine."
The place where these people lived is near Slater's Fork (Slaughter) which is in the south end of the county not many miles from the Virginia border. It seems that the settlers in this section were bothered more than some of the others because the Indians actually made their home in the Blue Ridge Mountains.

My grandfather Eager settled on Catron's Creek and had a large family of girls and the boy was the youngest. One time the girls were out early in the morning helping their father and mother away from the house and when they came in they knew the Indians had been there. They had taken all the iron pots and a coverlid in which they evidently carried the stuff away to their hiding place. The Eager girls got on mules and rode up the creek bed, tracking these Indians and found where they had made a fire and gone on to some other place, but had hidden the stolen things under a cliff. The girls gathered up the things and carried them back in the same coverlid the Indians took away with them and they were not molested by the Indians again.

There is the story of the Cornetts who came into Harlan because one of their relatives spied out the land while tracking Indians into Harlan County. It seems that a band of Indians had abducted a little girl in Virginia and a posse of men followed them through the mountains. When they got close on the heels of the Indians who were riding shod ponies, the Indians ran their ponies over a cliff near Poor Fork. One of the ponies was injured in the jump and in the confusion the Indians were delayed and outnumbered by the posse, so the white men recovered the little girl and took her back with them. People used to say that you could see the horseshoe rings where they marked the cliffs as they jumped from the cliffs.

The Indians who lived in Virginia and Tennessee had rather thickly populated villages. Berry Cawood, a Revolutionary soldier who came to Harlan County soon after the war, stated in his pension application that he served as an Indian fighter against the Cherokees. In 1776 during the campaign, they marched from Washington Co., passing Long Island Flats where lay the bodies of about 30 Indians recently killed in a battle with the whites. On this tour they burned Indian towns, he said. Indian corn was ripe, and there were plenty of pumpkins and sweet potatoes. "We burned three or four towns and ate up and destroyed all their corn, pumpkins and sweet potatoes." Another scout said that there was a good-sized Indian town in Virginia called French Town.

Several old persons who were born in the late eighteen forties have said that they recalled when the Indians were marched to the Indian Territory although some of them said it was Oklahoma Territory. At any rate the Indians were resettled and it is said that a few of them returned here. Possibly Sam Whitson is one of these who returned to Harlan County, or hid in the mountains as did the Cherokee Nation who stayed in the Smoky Mountains.

The Indian taught the white man many things, so there were some who were friendly at least part of the time. They told them where were the best hunting places, showed them how to raise corn and pound it into meal. They showed them how to raise sweet potatoes and pumpkins. They took them to the best fishing holes and showed them how to broil fish on tiny little fires between hot rocks. The recipe for scalded hoecakes is said to have been given to the white man by the Indians. That is one reason they liked to use iron pots for they needed pots to boil the water and skillets to fry the hoecakes. They knew all the herbs and showed them how to gather fruits and berries and to rob the bees of their honey.

CHAPTER XV

MILLING AND TRADES

THE grist mill could be called the lifeblood of the early days. It was a clearinghouse for news, gossip, crop talk, trading, swapping yarns and general information, and certainly it was the hub of the community.

When the corn was dry enough to grind in the fall, everyone went to mill as soon as possible. Their own meal supply was usually exhausted and they had to rely on fresh corn, roasting ears (rosenyears) and gritted bread. Gritted bread was made by grating the corn before it became hard enough to grind at the mill. It made a very moist, heavy bread, and even today there are folks who like to make gritted bread. Each farmer had to ride or use some kind of conveyance to get his turns of meal carried to the mill because a bushel was considered a "turn." Mules, horses, wagons and sleds would be hitched and parked all around the road to the mills during the grinding season. The miller retained one-eighth of the grain for his work and during the busy season, sacks would be piled high to the ceiling, tagged so the miller could identify the owner.

In this sparsely settled part of the country, the farmer, the merchant, the carpenter and the miller vied with each other for importance in the community. It is true that there were other businesses and professions, but these could hardly support a man and his family, unless he could raise enough to feed his family and the "critters." There were some fifteen or sixteen grist mills which are recalled and probably there were many hand mills at various farms. These hand mills were pounded by hand and could only supply a mess or so at a time when the family ran out of meal and could not get to the water mill. It was tedious and slow to pound by hand.

Probably one of the oldest mills is the River Mill which is in what is now Bell County. This mill was near the bend of the river below the present highway bridge at the intersection of the Harlan and Middlesboro-to-Pineville road, north of the Narrows. Farmers came to this mill from Strait Creek, down from Yellow Creek which was what Middlesboro was called in the old days, and from the section now called South America and from Wasioto. This was located on Boone Trail and was the heaviest traveled part of Harlan County.

Usually the millwright bought the rights on both banks of the river for a mile or so in order to be protected from having someone set up a mill too near him and decrease his water supply. In late summer and fall the river often got quite low and the miller could not get enough water to turn the wheel.

There was a mill at Cumberland Gap which was not far from Yellow Creek, now Middlesboro. There was a Goodman family who operated this mill about the time it was abandoned. It was located on the side of the mountain just about where the back end of the souvenir shop at Cudjo's Cave is located. This cave furnished a stream of very cold water and it is said the cave was called Cold Spring Cave and King Solomon's Cave. The water from this cave furnished power for a sawing mill which ground corn and wheat and also for woolens and flax. The merchants would send their raw wool to this mill and in return the merchants would receive a certain poundage of finished woolen coverlids in payment, with no money exchanged. When the railroad came to Middlesboro it is said that the channel of water flowing to their mill was changed and the mill was moved to Virginia. A Union soldier's diary which was printed in the Middlesboro *Daily News* on June 19, 1962, describes Cumberland Gap. "We found we were just at the foot of the Mt. Just below us was a big mill over shot, run by a big spring, the finest I ever saw. It runs three mills, a cording mill, grist and saw mill."

There was a mill owned by Jack Parsons referred to as Passon's Mill on Tan Yard Hill. The mill stones are still at the Parsons home which is about a mile or two east of the

MILLING AND TRADES

Calloway post office. The home the Parsons live in was the original home site of Lewis Green who built the chimneys that are still standing, and I understand the present house is the third one to use the same stone chimneys. The Parsons Mill got its water power from a log flume on the Pine Mountain side where the flume ran for about a half-mile from a stream on the mountain called Passon's Branch. These flumes were hand hewn out of split logs and took several months to laboriously fashion. This flume mill had the advantage over the milldam on the river because the Pine Mountain streams never ran dry and the miller could depend on power to run his wheel. The logs for the flume were so heavy it took several men to handle one log when joining it to its connecting log. This mill supplied the families on Browney's Creek, Pucketts Creek and Tan Yard or Tan Bark Hill up the river as far as Pace's Hill about where Coldiron is now, and at this place John R. Pace operated a mill at Pace's Hill.

Blanton's Mill was near Wallins on Jesse's Branch, located on the Pine Mountain side. There was a tub-wheel mill at Saylor's Creek near the foot of Pine Mountain below Wallins. Near the mouth of Poor Fork, on the left bank of the river going north from Baxter, there was a mill-dam, water-wheel grist mill operated by Martin Jones, known as Joneses Mill. There was a Huff Mill on the head of Poor Fork and it was called the Jim Huff Mill. At Clover Lick, near what is now Lynch, was a grist mill that supplied that end of the country as far as what is now Letcher County. A man named Felices ran this mill and lived at Poor Ford. It is not known whether this river was named for a man named Poore or whether the river was hard to ford at this place. It is now called Poor Fork.

Near the upper part of the Clover Fork River was a mill called Pounding Mill on Pounding Mill Creek. The pounding mill operated differently from the water-wheel power.

Most of the mill-stones had to be brought in to Harlan County from North Carolina because the stone in this county is not suitable for mill-stones.

The Holmes grist mill was on Clover Fork near Yokum

123

Creek. There was a grist mill on the mountain between Catron's Creek and Crank's Creek operated by Creed Smith. George Burkhart bought a mill in 1824 from James Farmer on Cranks Creek near the Aley Ledford line. The recorded contract mentions the millwright. On the mountain near Crummies Creek was a Spurlock Mill. Sol Pope willed his mill and mill field along with $150.00 to his son Babbat Pope. This was located on Catron's Creek.

On Martin's Fork was a grist mill known as Farmer's Mill and it is called Farmer's Mill today although the mill is no longer there. Stephen Farmer owned land on Martin's Fork and sold a parcel to Lewis Farmer, Sr., in 1823. Lewis

This 115 year old home was built in 1847 by John H. Farmer at Farmer's Mill. It is now owned by Ramsey and Jane Fulton Brock. (See page 36.) There were several men in the Farmer relations and with neighbors, they had a log rolling and log raising and shingle shake cutting to complete this dwelling in two days, according to tradition. Turn to page 36.

MILLING AND TRADES

Farmer married Anna Hensley on Sept. 25, 1836, with Luke Noe the preacher. W. C. Farmer married Catherin Fannie Branson Dec. 14, 1846, with Hiram Lewis the preacher. Stephen Farmer married Jane Fee in 1842 by Preacher George Spurlock. James Farmer married Susan Skidmore November 1850. John H. Farmer married Rebecca Jane Ledford June 20, 1847, with Noble Smith the preacher. They built a log home with hand hewn logs and "shake" shingles. In 1947 Ramsey Brock and wife Jane Fulton Brock bought this hundred-year-old home and restored it as much as possible.

Lewis Farmer, Jr., married Ellen Rice with witnesses Isom Skidmore and Lewis Farmer (probably his father) on Nov. 1, 1870. His brother Sherman Farmer remained in Harlan but Lewis and his wife went to California to take up a claim about fifteen miles from Los Angeles. Had he not been a carpenter by trade, they could never have survived. They planted their ranch in English walnuts which took several years to produce a crop. The second year it bore a crop the shells were damaged by cold weather and were too thin to ship. The enterprising daughters cracked the nut meats out and took a box full in to a confectioner in Los Angeles to see if he would buy the nut meats. He was pleased to get the nuts already shelled and told them he would take all that they could bring in to him. Their crop failure turned out to be a success and it is likely this started the idea of selling nut meats instead of the whole unshelled nuts.

There was a grist mill near Smith called the Hall Mill, run by Alford Hall, Sr.

The Ben A. Rice grist mill was erected in the town of Harlan after the Civil War. A milldam was built across the Clover Fork River, just east of the present bridge, with all the necessary millwrights for two miles on both sides of the river. He also had an attachment to saw lumber with the same power that furnished the grist mill. The lumber sawed at this mill was used to build the third courthouse which was of frame construction and a two-story frame jailhouse. This mill furnished lumber for many of the frame houses which

This grist mill had a sawing attachment which sawed the lumber for the frame courthouse, built after the brick courthouse burned during the Civil War. The frame courthouse can be seen over the top of the mill to the right. The dam was built above the old Cow Ford where a path led through the fields across the Clover Fork River which is now Main Street.

were built in Harlan up until about 1895. The grist mill was carried on by his son Henry Clay Rice who sold it to Judge W. C. L. Huff about 1910, and his son, Hamp Huff, operated it with a gasoline attachment up until the late nineteen thirties when it was abandoned. Ben A. Rice ordered the first store-bought mantel in southeastern Kentucky and people came for miles to look at it.

There was some buckwheat raised in this county as well as a little soft wheat. The wheat which was ground was very dark—a sort of reddish brown—and was reserved for Sunday morning biscuit and gingerbread at Thanskgiving and Christmas. My father said his mother always made biscuits on Sunday morning which the children all looked forward to eating with butter and molasses, honey or maple syrup. The wheat flour was called "shorts" and it had all the natural flavor and nutrition in it. The buckwheat was used mostly for flapjacks which were served with honey, molasses or maple syrup.

The wheat flour and meal easily became moldy or sour or became infested with weevils in the summertime; therefore a great quantity could not be kept on hand at one time although it took a lot of grain to feed the stock, chickens and the family.

MILLING AND TRADES

Homemade products from the farm made business by bartering or swapping. Every farmer had a beestand and sold honey. From the comb beeswax produced a good business. Sorghum or molasses was another good product which took a lot of work besides "raisin' cane." When the cane was ripe it had to be cut and then ground into a vat which caught the juice. Then this juice had to be boiled down for hours while someone kept the fire at the right temperature. A "stiroff" was attended by all the neighbors who lent a helping hand and made a social event out of it. Long ladles drew off the foam as it boiled and then the children were allowed to lick the sweet sticky juice when the ladle cooled. When boiled down to the right thickness the sorghum was stored in crocks and vessels. Care had to be used to keep the syrup from scorching because that would hurt the flavor.

Maple sugar was another industry which was a lot of work. The trees had to be tapped at the right time to catch the sap when it was "right." Then the sap had to be boiled down to make either syrup or, because it was easier to store, sugar, which was molded in various sizes for easy handling.

Clay bricking kilns were also needed and here in Harlan the brickyard was a clay hill between the present Methodist Church and Dr. W. P. Cawood's home at Mound and Main Streets. Pottery was not made by the settlers although it is said that the Indians used to make pottery. There is an old saying that where dirt daubers build their nest then you can use that clay for brick or pottery.

Wool was a very good business if a man could raise more than he needed for his own use, although it took a good bit of wool to make all the clothing for the family and covers for the beds. Merchants accepted raw wool in exchange for "boughten" goods, and the merchant took the wool to a commercial mill where the woolen miller kept his percent and then sent the merchant woven loom coverlids which he then offered for sale in his store.

Most of the farmers raised tobacco for their own use but did not sell much in this county, although tobacco was reckoned as good as sterling in payment.

Chapter XVI

BUSINESS AND BANKING

THERE were many varieties of business that the pioneer learned to do himself because there was not enough demand to set up some kinds of businesses. For instance, the barber, doctor, schoolmaster, barrister, cobbler, blacksmith and leather worker usually had to farm or do other work to make enough to live on. There were jobs of smithing, tinning, harness making, saddlers, belts, whips, in connection with other work. Then there were the stone mason, woodworker, axeman, title surveyor, rodman, compass-man and many jobs which had to be combined. At this early date the women usually made all the clothing, from spinning, weaving, tayloring (tailoring) men's clothes, as well as ladies' and children's dresses and bonnets. Even the preacher usually had to help out by farming or perhaps he could do carpenter work.

The postmaster had an enviable position because people looked up to the man who handled the mail. When someone wanted to write a letter to a faraway relative, he would ask the postmaster to "back" the address on the envelope for them.

Letters addressed to the town of Mount Pleasant in 1878 were properly sent to Harlan Court House, Harlan County, Ky. Though the county seat remained Mount Pleasant, the post office address was Harlan Court House.

Tan Yard Hill was so named because there was a tannery on the mountain. It formerly was called Tan Bark Hill due to wood bark used to make potash lye to soak the skin of animals. In the curing process, a stench arose from the vats which was noticeable for miles around. When the skins were finished curing, they were hauled to the Settlements at Lexington and exchanged for goods which the mountaineers needed.

Lewis Green came to the Cumberland River before 1800 and dug these vats to use in the curing of hides and it is said that it is the first tannery in this section. He had six sons and four daughters who married and lived near that section between Pucketts Creek and Browney's Creek. The family did all the work and when a load of skins were ready, they were piled on oxen sleds and taken to the Settlements to trade. This trip was slow and it took several weeks to make the round trip.

The carpenter had to be on his own because up until about the time the frame houses began to be built, a carpenter could not make a living working for other folks but every man had to be a carpenter on his own. Some people were adept at fashioning wooden vessels and implements but in the very early days a carpenter had to supplement his work with other jobs.

The early merchant was a retailer, wholesaler, jobber and trader. There was little money and most everything was bartered. It would take a merchant several weeks to make a round trip to the settlements, taking along raw goods such as hides, ginseng, snake root, beeswax, wool, feathers, maple sugar, honey, cured meats and anything which could be sold. The merchant would bring things to his store which the mountaineer could not make at home such as steel needles, cotton thread, cotton goods, silk, lamp oil, patterns, steel cutlery and coffee which was green, unroasted and came in bushel sacks. The green coffee had to be roasted and ground at home. Spice, pepper, mace, coffee, cinnamon and cream of tartar were simple luxuries.

The general store played an important part in the life of the early settlers. The building was made with a wide, high front porch to facilitate loading and unloading from the wagons which could pull up to the porch level somewhat like the wholesale houses have now. In fact, it seems to me it would be mighty handy now if the trucks could pull up to a loading platform to unload their deliveries.

Business was not carried on in the manner of today because the customers had to spend a few hours in town and chairs were kept on the porch in summer for the men to sit on and talk, whittle and spin yarns. In winter they moved inside and sat around a potbellied stove where most of them chewed tobacco and their spit sizzled on the hot stove as they talked and listened to tales of bygone days as well as news headlines of the day.

J. H. Spurlock who was born in 1828 was a merchant in 1860 on Martin's Fork. Calico, gingham and lawn were among the most desirable items because cotton was not raised in the mountains. Dress patterns came already measured in lengths of seven yards which it took to make a dress at that time. Silk patterns were usually ordered for a special customer because silk was not common in the early days.

In 1887 there were about ten stores in Mount Pleasant doing business. John Jones, who married Martha Creech, had a store about where the Bowling Building now stands. Her father, Ezekiel Creech, from Hancock County, Tenn., was a hatmaker by trade and was known as "Hatter Creech." A. W. Couk had a large store where Watson's now is, and he sent out the first calendar in town. Other merchants were T. S. (Grandaddy) Ward, Jerome Skidmore, brother to Daniel and Lafayette Harris whose store was located about where the Baptist Church now stands.

Jonathan K. Bailey had a store about where the Court Cafe is now and Sam Clay Howard had a store and hotel at the corner of Central and Second. Hiram Cawood had a store at Cawood. A Saylor, a Taylor and a Blanton had stores at Wallins. Adrian Nolan had a store at Nolan's Branch; Joe Blair and Ab Howard had stores on Poor Fork. One of the Smiths had a store at Evarts and W. B. Kelly had a store on Yokum Creek. Cam Ball had a store at Pansy, Sol Buckhart had a store on Cranks Creek and Alford Hall one on Martin's Fork.

Walter Z. Gregory was the first undertaker in Mount Pleasant because he was the first store owner who handled "store-boughten" coffins about 1889.

A few people built ice houses, filled with sawdust, and when ice froze over on the river, it was sawed and packed in the sawdust. Sometimes the ice would last until up in July and even then it was usually kept for sick folks.

BUSINESS AND BANKING

Each man was a volunteer fire fighter and anyone would help fight fire because sudden winds and heat could easily make a bonfire get out of control. However, they were all fire-conscious and were as careful as could be when burning brush or using fires for any reason.

Matches were not common and when a person built a fire out of doors, he usually carried red-hot coals in an iron vessel to start a fire. Or he would use a wooden squib, lighted, or a wooden-stick poker with a burning end which would light the necessary fire. However, the wooden squib could not be carried more than a few feet for safety's sake.

One of their most fascinating businesses was also a pastime and sideline, that of "haws tradin'," "haws racin'," and "haws raisin'." There were four race tracks in the county at one time which would be considered private but people brought their horses and came on certain days to race, trade, and watch. I know where two of these tracks were but the other two are not known to me. On Brittain's Hill, George Brittain of Martin's Fork had a famous three-storied stable with a ground level for each floor built on an Indian Mound. The track stretched out to the river about where the Memorial Hospital is now. When a man placed his horse in a race he agreed with the other owner that if his horse was not the best horse (which he always believed it was) then the winner would claim his horse. Perhaps this is the origin of the Claiming Races.

Jack McGeorge and Colonel Bill Green had a mile and a half race track in the bottom land stretching from Tan Bark Hill to the Cumberland River. It is said that they won and lost as much as $10,000 (mostly lost) on a horse they called Ditto. Young Negro boys were both jockeys and grooms and loved everything about taking care of the horses and racing. One little boy was so small that they thought he could not ride in a race. One day he put resin on his britches so he could stick on the horse so that he could ride in the race. The whole countryside would be filled with horsemen, horse-traders and horsey people on the day set for certain places to race. It is said many a blind horse was swapped off on a racing day.

Hampton Lewis, who married first Emily Howard, lived about halfway between Pineville and Harlan, and his home was called the "Halfway House." This was considered a good stopping place where they fed you and could bed you down for the night. However, on racing days, they could hardly keep enough food cooked to feed the crowds that came to the races. This did not count folks who could visit their relatives for free.

About the time the Civil War was over there was a good bit of activity on account of people drilling for salt. Up until this time the people here had to go over through Goose Creek to Clay County at Manchester to get salt. They had salt wells where they boiled down the water to make salt. Now the lawyer came into his own. Individuals and companies made contracts and leases for drilling for salt rights, including oil, coal, iron or other minerals. It was said that Murph Ward on Strait Creek was drilling for salt and found a sticky substance which we now believe was oil. Here in Harlan were drillers who leased the salt rights in what is now Georgetown addition to Harlan, then a hayfield. Not long after this, salt was shipped commercially to the stores and so the salt drilling was abandoned.

In the early eighties the lumber business began to be a real stimulus to the mountaineers. Three big lumber companies came into Harlan—two from Williamsburg, The Jones Lumber Company the Williamsburg Lumber Company, and the T. J. Asher Lumber Company, Wasioto. They employed more people than any one type of business probably had up to this time. When payday came most of the men were paid off in cash because there was no bank here then. Each company had a brand at the end of his logs either with dots, dashes or an "x" so the logs could be separated later but during highwater all the logs floated down the river and it was a sight to see and hear those logs boom-booming in the churning waters. Occasionally the lumberjacks had to go out with big cant hooks and unjam the logs which

BUSINESS AND BANKING

would get caught at times and pile up on each other. This was dangerous and exciting for others to watch these men walk the rolling logs in the whirling water. This business employed lawyers, abstractors, surveyors, line men, axemen, and woodsmen. There was a narrow-gauge incline built up Pine Mountain to carry logs to the river. There were times when they would let picnickers ride the empty flat cars and that became a great pastime with the young folks.

About 1888 the photographic business began to flourish in the county. In the very early days, many a child has been punished for drawing cartoons and caricatures on his slate. They were told to stick to birds and animals or even whittle if they would. The talent any child might have had was erased with the next slate full. When the early pioneers made a trip to any settlement, it never occurred to them to carry a painting even if it were their own folks, so I guess there never was a painting here in the early days. There was an attempt to outline a face in cross-stitching, and even in large cities, engravings and tapestries were the only likenesses other than paintings. It seems that over in France, Niepce and Daguerre were working with metallic plates with the help of sunlight to hold an imprint. In Germany and England scientists were also working on this, but Daguerre got the credit for this. By 1870 even as isolated as is Harlan County, there were many tintypes of families in most of the homes. After the photographic glass plate was perfected, the Harlan folks had sittings at the gallery. The first photographic gallery was started here by two sisters, Mrs. George T. Howard who was Nan Smith and Mrs. W. Boyd Kelly who was Margaret Smith. Here the young folks liked to loaf, gossip and visit and it became the meeting place of the young set. Later they sold their business to Mrs. J. S. Bailey (Mollie Ball) and the name was changed to the Harlan Photo Gallery.

The old-fashioned drummer would be what you might call a sales engineer. The drummer went through the country, riding, walking or hitching a ride, and stopped at every house and store that he could. He was the wholesaler, canvasser and retailer.

Once a watch and clock salesman named Charles Calloway came riding through the country, and he met and married a girl named Elizabeth Green, daughter of Nancy Gardner Green and James Green. They moved to Cawood to live and their daughter Virginia married Stephen Cawood.

Later that invention, the lightning rods on homes, was sold to homeowners by drummers. I thought a house with lightning rods on it was proof of high living. We did not have any; papa was a merchant.

My great-grandmother bought a pair of spectacles from a salesman and he carried along a few pair which he fitted and a magazine for her to read to test them. Magazines and periodicals were scarce in those days so very few people had them, and they probably never saw a newspaper. Anyway the house my great-grandmother lived in burned about 1900 and she lost her glasses. Since she could not replace the glass, she began to read and sew without spectacles and regained her second eyesight enough to thread a needle and read and weave.

There was the furniture or lathe worker who went through the country with his equipment and he would stop at a farm house. If they would keep him through the winter and let him make beds, tables, chairs and things, he charged a nominal sum. Many of the old spool beds, spinning wheels and chairs were made out of wood cured around the fireplace with the help of the latheworker. At the same time the youngsters learned a little about the art of furniture making.

Tailoring had long been done in the home, usually the women making the suits worn by the men, and it was all done by hand. Where women were situated so they could do so, they would "take in" sewing for other people. My grandmother ordered the first sewing machine in Mount Pleasant about 1876 which she bought from a man named Sloan, a drummer who was the agent for Wheeler and Wilson, at a cost of $100.00. She took in enough sewing the first year to pay for the machine. A Mrs. Blackburn and her mother, a Mrs. Hinkle, bought a sewing machine and did sewing for other people.

BUSINESS AND BANKING

About 1890 the millinery business flourished in town and an ambitious girl would learn to make hats to sell to other people. It took a little capital to buy the material and frames to work with and the girl needed to go to the "city" to a wholesale house to learn to trim and make hats, but when she learned the millinery business she could make a living.

Surveying was an important job from the very early days and the county appointed a surveyor. Jonathan Smith was the County Surveyor in 1845 and lived on Poor Fork. Later as land titles, abstracts and leases became more numerous, surveyors were doing a good business.

Blacksmithing became so important that James B. Smith, from Poor Fork, ran the first one in Harlan; later Henry Creech, colored, operated one where the swimming pool is at Elm and Central.

After the railroad came up through Virginia, Hagan was our nearest shipping point. Henry Clay Rice opened a livery stable where he rented horses by the day or hour to out of town riders and he kept a relay station at Hagan. He kept mule teams and wagons which he rented for drovers who picked up freight and express and carried them back to Harlan. These teamsters, or drovers, had to be strong, sturdy, reliable men who could handle a loaded wagon over rough roads.

There had long been the need for a newspaper in this county and about 1900 a man named James Eads came here and published a paper he called *The Enterprise* or *The Harlan Enterprise*, I am not sure which name, and I think it was a weekly paper. It is now the same paper we look forward to daily called *The Harlan Daily Enterprise*.

There had long been a need for a bank here in Harlan. Banking business had to be done as far away as Jonesville, Va., or at the settlements down in the State, and later the Pineville Banking Co. My father and a man named Lee Creech who both had stores each owned a steel-iron safe, painted black. One time Milton Jones, father of Dr. J. B. Jones, sold a tract of land and was paid $10,000 in cash

Will W. Noe's General Store—Corner of Central and Second Streets. He and his wife Margie Lewis Noe owned the store and building which housed the first bank, now the Margie Grand Theatre Building. She was the daughter of Judge Wilson Lewis and Fannia Jones Lewis. Fannia Jones was the daughter of Hiram and Rachel Ely Jones and he was the son of Stephen Jones, the Revolutionary soldier.

Standing in front of the store is William Wadsworth Lewis, first cashier of the First State Bank, later County Judge. He was a descendant of Jesse Brock, the Revolutionary soldier. His parents were Felix Goldwin Lewis and Mary Blanton Lewis. His first wife was Ollie Cornett, daughter of Arthur Blankenship Cornett and Ella Amanda Hurst Cornett.

which he asked my father to put in his safe for safekeeping. My father did keep it in his safe for several months until Mr. Jones could go to a bank but the responsibility weighed heavily for keeping such a sum of money.

About 1901 a group of businessmen here in the county met and decided to form a bank. The capital stock was $15,000; each officer and director subscribed for stock—

W. W. Noe was the President ....15 shares

BUSINESS AND BANKING

G. W. Green was the Vice-President .... 10 shares
Will W. Lewis was the Cashier .... 10 shares

Directors
Sam C. Howard .... 10 shares
F. G. Lewis .... 10 shares
Dave Vahenger .... 10 shares
J. B. Lewis .... 10 shares
C. B. Pope .... 10 shares
A. B. Cornett .... 10 shares

Stockholders
W. A. Brock .... 5 shares
W. W. Cornett .... 5 shares
R. N. Cornett .... 11 shares
P. B. Howard .... 10 shares
Chas. Hall .... 5 shares
H. L. Howard .... 2 shares
M. R. Howard .... 2 shares
F. S. Hensley .... 5 shares
B. F. & A. Z. Kelly .... 2 shares
M. D. Smith .... 5 shares
T. F. Ward .... 3 shares

In 1902 the First State Bank was incorporated and it earned money the first year. The officers then were
W. W. Noe .... President
Dave Vahenger .... Vice-President
W. W. Lewis .... Cashier
M. R. Howard .... Asst. Cashier

The capital stock was raised to $20,000 with Charles Henry Davis of South Yarmouth, Mass., adding $5,000.00.

Chapter XVII

TRAVEL AND COMMUNICATIONS

THERE were many hardships suffered by these early pilgrims hunting for the promised land. There was a story told of a young couple with a baby in arms who sold all their possessions to buy an ox team and cart to start westward through Kentucky. When they came to the rough road near Cumberland Gap, the wife decided to walk ahead and carry the baby for fear they would be jolted off the cart. Somehow the oxen were scared by something and got out of control and in trying to get out of their way the young mother's baby was knocked from her arms and crushed by the team. There the baby was buried in an unmarked grave and the couple had to continue on their trip.

My own great-grandmother and her husband started to Indiana and had to go to Cloverport to Ferry which was about 20 miles below the falls at Louisville, Ky. On their way, they lost two children by death who are buried somewhere on the road to Indiana. They turned back after this sad experience and came to Harlan County and settled.

My grandfather and grandmother went to Kansas and took up a claim about 1880. The dry winds ruined their crop. They were living in a dugout and had to burn dried buffalo chips for fuel so they became dissatisfied and returned to Harlan County to live. However, they did buy an iron cookstove, I think in St. Louis, the first one my grandmother had ever cooked on, and she was very pleased with it.

Communications and transportation were primitive in the early days of Harlan County. The very earliest scouts traveled light and had only a pack on their back, a gun and a knife or ax.

There were a few choices for the early settlers, one, "shanks mares" which is simply your own legs. A few riders could stay mounted on a steer; others had mules or horses to ride. For narrow trails there was the oxcart and when the trails

TRAVEL AND COMMUNICATIONS

were improved, the sled drawn by oxen and the jolt wagon usually pulled by mules. Later there was occasionally a buckboard or a hack, but the buggy and surrey would not hold up on rough mountain roads.

The Boone Trail, which went through Cumberland Gap via Cumberland Ford (Pineville) and on to the Blue Grass Country, was the most traveled road and after Boone blazed the trail, others improved it until by the time the Civil War came, covered wagons and other vehicles made the trip. Both the Yanks and the Rebels worked on the road leading to Cumberland Gap and by the time the Civil War was over, it was quite passable, having been filled in where there were large holes. Where the road crossed creeks and stayed muddy and mucky corduroy or cordwood roads were made by laying large logs lengthwise and then another layer of large logs laid crosswise. There were remnants of this cordwood road near the old freight depot at Pineville as late as the early nineteen hundreds.

Boone Trail was the first national highway, which started in Maryland and extended through what was then Harlan County. The road between Cumberland Gap and Pineville Ford was rough and steep as it crossed the mountain at the Gap and then through Yellow Creek country which is now Middlesboro, and Big Log Mountain and Little Log Mountain had to be crossed before reaching Wasioto on the Cumberland River and on to the Narrows near Cumberland Ford. The high steep rocky cliff on each side of the river at this point narrowed the width of the river and got the name of The Narrows.

Fording the Cumberland River at the Cumberland Ford, which is now Pineville, was impossible during floods and high water. The travelers had to wait for two or three days until they could get across and sometimes there would be wagons, vehicles, animals, riders and walking folks waiting to be "set" across the river. Most of them were prepared to camp along the way but their "victuals" often ran low so it was only natural that the sparsely settled country would have some farmers who could furnish food and lodging. The

139

animals needed to be fed as well as the families of these travelers who waited in the long caravan for their turn to cross the river. Some of the daring travelers would swim their animals across the swollen stream and often lost their belongings in so doing.

It was natural for the Ferry to be established at this point. At one time the Ferry was operated by J. J. Gibson but I do not know the name of the man who bought the franchise. The rate for ferrying across was 5¢ for a horse, 15¢ for one horse with wagon and a covered wagon with more than one horse was fifty cents. There was a story told in connection with the river crossing at Cumberland Ford. The people who lived on the north side of the Cumberland River were preparing a wedding feast for their daughter who was getting married. A great crowd of friends and well-wishers had gathered for the ceremony and to enjoy the good food which was ready to serve the guests. In the meantime, the river got up so high it became past fording or swimming the animals on account of a dangerous current and the groom was water-bound on the other side. There were travelers at this lodging house who were not able to get across the river so one of the young men in this group asked to see the bride. He liked her looks and she liked him and then and there they went through the wedding ceremony with the original plans except for the groom. As far as I know they lived happily ever after.

The would-be-groom was left high and dry on the other side and I knew him. His name was Jeff Hoskins and later he married Lucy Renfro and they had a nice family. Lucy Renfro was the daughter of a widow, Susan Birch Renfro, who married James Renfro and he died young. I shall tell you a story about her in another chapter.

The Hoskins children were: Suzie who married a Gregg, Joe, Carl, Ruth and John. John became something of a notable during World War II when he got the nickname of "Long John."

In ordinary times the boat and canoe were the means of getting across the river, although there were times when the water was so low one could walk across a shoals on rocks and

TRAVEL AND COMMUNICATIONS

hardly get one's feet wet. Canoe and boat landings were made with the permission, lease or contract with the person owning the landing. Of course some of the landowners held land on each side of the river; otherwise they had to get a landing privilege with ingress and egress over the other fellow's land.

The milldams which were built across the rivers for grist mills served as a very good walking bridge in dry weather and this was done with permission of the millwright.

The hired horse is practically a forerunner of the cab or taxi of today. The livery stable was as fascinating to the young fry as the bus depots and airports are today. Many of the young boys hung around the stable for hours hoping to get to help and earn a few pennies. There was always extra work around the stable with the horses having to be taken to the river to be watered and usually young boys would do this chore just to get to learn to ride. Occasionally they would get to carry a man's grip to his hotel or if the man rode to the hotel maybe the man would let him bring the horse back to the stable and pay him a nickle. More often the rider would fasten the bridle to the saddle and slap the horse and the horse would go to the stable all by himself.

Charlie Smith, son of Dave and Susan Smith, loved horses and he used to work at the livery stable, taking care of the horses and saddling up for the riders. He got the nickname of "Sad" Smith which many of the older men called him even after the livery stable was out of date.

The livery stable became important to the early traveler because some came with other parties as far as the mountains and from there one went one way and the other went "tother" way. In which case a traveler would rent a horse by the hour, day or week. There was not much risk in hiring a horse out to a stranger because horsestealing was considered just about the very meanest crime that could be done; therefore the consequences were dire doom for the horse thief.

The livery stables also kept mules and teams to rent out for people who hauled freight and express to the settlements.

In earlier days a farmer or a merchant kept a team of oxen with sled or wagon to haul goods from as far off as Lexington, Ky., or Jonesville, Va. It took weeks to make this kind of trip but it was the only way of shipping out raw goods and bringing in "store-boughten" goods.

The livery man would often hire a lad to deliver a horse to a certain party many miles from the stable, and then the boy would walk back unless the man who hired the horse would let him ride behind him double. Some horses would not accept a double passenger. Orville Howard and Hobart Howard, sons of Henry L. Howard, Commonwealth's attorney at that time, said they used to take horses to Cawood to meet men who had come on the train to the Virginia station and the men had sent word to meet them with horses. The boys were paid 25¢ each for this job and many a time they had to walk back because the men did not always let them ride behind them back to town.

The earliest freight lines went all the way to Lexington, Ky., called the settlements, and that was usually by oxen team. Then as the railroad came farther up the east, the freight was hauled from Broadhead and Livingston and later from Woodbine, which is near Corbin, and then to Pineville after the L&N Railroad came to the mountains. After the trains began running up to Norton, then the freight and express as well as passengers used Hagan and Pennington Gap, Va., as their destination to begin the rough trip over the mountain to Harlan. The roads were precipitous over the stone mountain and at times a loaded wagon would be almost on its side end crossing a high boulder. The teamsters had to not only know how to handle the team but also had to judge the best way to go over the rough spots. Usually there were other teamsters driving at the same time and when a wagon broke down, they had to be a good enough mechanic to fix it. They were the forerunners of the modern Trailer-Truck-Van drivers.

When riding horseback the rider had to be careful about letter a horse drink too much when crossing a stream, and the women who rode a side-saddle had to hold on to keep from falling over the horse's neck when he leaned down to drink.

TRAVEL AND COMMUNICATIONS

A woman who was crossing the river, with her small daughter in her lap, dropped the child in the river because she could not hold on to the child, the bridle and the side-saddle when the horse suddenly leaned his neck down to drink. Fortunately, the child was not hurt and the water was shallow and a sandy bottom at this spot where she was fording the river.

Communications were slow, due to people having to send word by a messenger.

I recall that a young dentist, Harmon Eager, died in another county and his body was about a week on the rough road when they brought him back for burial.

When trade opened up following the Civil War, flour was shipped in to Harlan and a hundred pound barrel cost $5.00.

Light brown sugar, raw sugar and dark brown sugar were shipped in large barrels and were weighed out to the customer by scooping out the sugar into a container which the customer brought along with him. The container was weighed before the sugar was put into it so the merchant could tell how much sugar would weigh.

A nickel's worth of brown sugar, cheese and crackers was more than one person could eat for a snack at lunch time and could be bought at any of the stores.

Crackers were shipped in bulk in large wooden boxes called "loose" crackers and the merchant counted out as many as one wanted.

Cheese came in large "heads" which the merchant sliced off at the customer's order.

Salt was one of the most precious commodities in the earliest days. It was hard to come by because the settlers had to form a party to go over into Clay County to the Salt Mines, by way of Goose Creek and Greasy Creek and Red Bird River country, or through Middlefork and Leatherwood. This trip was done in the Fall of the year and the men tried to carry back enough salt to last a year. It took about three bushels of salt to run a family through to the next season, including stock and cattle. When the salt supply was exhausted, the family had to do without until the next trip.

The women prepared large strong bags and the men took skins to protect the filled bags of salt to keep it dry on the return trip. Each man carried his ax, knife, hunting rifle and powder because they must camp along the way and provide their own food. In case of accident, it took two men to carry a wounded man on an improvised litter, hammock style, made from skins stretched on two sapling poles. On the return trip the men carried the salt bags, secured on long sapling poles, one man holding one end of the pole on his shoulder and the other man carrying the other end of the pole on his shoulder. This way, two men could carry six bushel bags, where one man could only handle one bushel bag on his back. It took several days to complete the trip and it was considered a very dangerous undertaking on account of wild animals. Some men who started out never lived to see home and family again. At night, the men kept a campfire going and each man took his turn at watch. If a man could provide a pack mule for the trip, it was not used for riding because the men walked. The road leading northwest into Clay County was known as Salt Trace and it is still called by that name. Until this year of 1962 there was a one-room schoolhouse known as the Salt Trace School and it has been abandoned. Salt Trace is still a voting precinct, though the post office is Bledsoe. Up until the Civil War, this trail was used to carry salt, but soon after the war, salt began to be shipped commercially and the trip into Clay County for salt was not necessary.

Communications were slow and the mail was delayed by weather and highwater ofttimes. A telegram was sent to the nearest telegraph office and was delivered by mail when the mailman arrived. The mailman got through even though snow and sleet delayed his arrival in bad weather. He rode a mule or horse and carried the mail in large saddlebags and often an extra pouch tied on behind his saddle.

In 1903 a group of businessmen got together and decided to organize a telephone company and the stockholders were:

| M. D. Smith | C. B. Pope | W. R. Maupin |
| W. W. Eager | S. M. Cawood | W. E. Garrett |

TRAVEL AND COMMUNICATIONS

R. G. Eager	Geo. T. Cawood	Gilbert Saylor
Grant Smith	N. S. Howard	F. H. Brittain
J. W. Smith	D. S. Farmer	L. H. Baylor
G. A. Eager	W. H. H. Smith	

Mrs. Grant Smith, whom everyone called Mary Grant, was the first telephone operator. This office was upstairs over the store of the Ball Brothers, Daniel and Cam Ball, where the Modern Electric Furniture store now is.

The Harlan Telephone Company moved its office to a small cottage on First Street where Charlie Howard's home is located. Mrs. Malinda Blair Johnson, who was a widow, lived there and operated the switchboard. Later Mrs. Alice Smith Middleton became the operator and one time a fellow from Cincinnati tried to phone a girl he knew and Miss Alice told him that the girl wasn't at home that day because she saw her going to a party. He was intrigued with this small-town way of knowing what everyone in town was doing.

Up until the time of the telephone, people here did not greet you with "hello"; the hello followed the convenience of the telephone.

The newspapers and publications had to be carried in by the mail man along with first class mail. It was not until 1901 that Mr. Jim Eads came here and started the first newspaper, *The Harlan Enterprise*. People still subscribed for some out-of-town publications. *The Courier Journal* had long been a favorite paper with many of the old-timers. It used to be a magazine-sized periodical and a man named James Shuttleworth said he peddled it between Louisville and Danville and charged 50¢ a copy for his trouble. John A. Ward used to work under James Shuttleworth and he named one of his sons James Shuttleworth Ward.

Lodging accommodations for travelers is as old as history. In Harlan County it was mostly the homes where room was stretched to take care of a traveler. Many travelers carried their own blanket and only asked for room to sleep on the floor. Lodging accommodations did not start out as a business; like Topsy it just "growed."

At Cumberland Gap there was a "stopping" place and at Cumberland Ford near the Narrows there was a place on each side of the river bank where folks could stop for rest. Business must have become bustling there because some days there were almost endless caravans of wagons and carts waiting to cross the river. At Clear Creek a family named the Calve Smiths could keep folks overnight and the Tom Gibson home was said to have taken in lodgers. Later the Ferry was operated by a Gibson and he may have been his son J. J. Gibson.

The Halfway House at Tanyard Hill run by Hampton and Emily Lewis has been mentioned. There were places up and down all the Forks which could take in travelers. The Kelly place at Evarts was a stopping place and on Poor Fork the Creech place as well as the Nolans and the Lewises. Abner Lewis on Pine Mountain was a good place to spend the night and on Martin's Fork the Burkharts, Smiths and Spurlocks. On Catron's Creek one could stay with the Joneses, the Noes

Frame hotel stood where is now the Bank of Harlan across from Green-Mill at Central and First Streets. *Left to right:* Rev. Carl T. Michel, Prof. Abner C. Jones, Judge Will L. Bailey, Judge Moses Wilkerson Howard, Judge Edward Sampson, Judge W. W. Lewis, John Blair, Inn Keeper, John Blanton Lewis, Will W. Noe, Sheriff Hamp H. Howard, Dick Fish, George W. Green.

and the Henry Smith farm. Not far from town Colonel George Brittain had the most well-known place to stay.

At the turn of the century there were several rooming and boarding houses in Mount Pleasant. Sam C. Howard had an imposing building which was a store and hotel on the corner from the courthouse. John Blair ran the old Harlan Hotel which was on the corner where the Bank of Harlan is now located. Joe Kelly had a hotel where the Cumberland Valley Music Company and Quality Shop is now located, and before that he had a frame hotel on Main Street. G. W. Green named his house "The Imperial" and was the first person to serve in individual dishes. This was at the north end of the post office and was later converted into the Shady Lawn Hospital.

Usually the food was served country style on long tables in most of the eating places and the filled dishes were placed on the table for each and everyone to serve his own plate. This custom prevailed until around 1900 in this part of the country but in the East some of the big hotels used a hand-written bill-of-fare from which one could order as one pleased. These hand-written bills-of-fare appeared sometime about 1850 in the American hotels, before menus were used in the old country.

Chapter XVIII

MEDICINE

THE care of the teeth was quite different then from what it is today. People did use toothbrushes, with the help of salt or sand to clean their teeth. The brush was a little twig broken from a green branch with the end chewed until it was brushy at one end, or a toothpick was whittled from a branch and discarded later. The quill toothpick was quite elegant and many of the old inns had a small holder with a quill sharpened at one end for their guests. Not too long ago, at a banquet, favors were individually wrapped quill toothpicks, a reminder of earlier days.

It is said that chewing tobacco was good for the teeth and gums, although it discolored the teeth. When one got the toothache, there were many remedies, from a dram of "likker" to a "chaw of bakker." These remedies failing, there was nothing to resort to except the farm pliers, unless there was a physician nearby. Then there was no way to replace the loss of a permanent tooth and the person went without and became "snaggle toothed."

I have read that General Washington had trouble with his teeth and when he lost one, he would try to whittle a tooth out of white wood and wire it to his other teeth. I have also heard that he tried to wire carved ivory for a tooth which he tried to tie on to his good ones.

It is said that in larger communities where there was a barber that the barber was a doctor of many ailments and that he kept pliers on hand to get rid of his customer's tooth troubles. Whiskey was the only anesthetic in the early days, and salt was the only antiseptic.

When the children started losing their baby teeth, usually some of the grownups or the older children would tie a string on the loose tooth and yank it out.

If the teeth did not come out straight then there was no method of straightening them, and they sometimes grew

MEDICINE

back crooked or protruding which was something which could not be helped at that time.

The first dentist I knew was Dr. J. T. Walker, who married Miss Mattie Riddle. Up until he located in Mount Pleasant, the doctors took care of teeth. As far as I know, there were no other dentists in Harlan County. He came here about 1890 and opened an office.

The old-timers used to say they had attacks of scurvy in the wintertime when there were no fresh vegetables. However, they did keep cabbage, potatoes and apples through the winter and practically everyone made kraut which was packed in wooden vessels or stone crocks.

Physicians were scarce and far between, but according to the 1850 census, there was a Dr. James Huff and his wife Obedience living in Harlan County. Both were born in Virginia and old people said that they had heard of a Dr. Huff who lived near Cumberland Ford (now Pineville) as early as 1800.

Dr. Nimrod Dawson, son of Williams Dawson, practiced medicine before the Civil War near Cumberland Ford. Dr. Judah Harris, who was born in 1790, practiced midwifery during the Civil War.

About the time of the Civil War, or before, there were Dr. John Mills and Dr. John B. Lyttle, who was born in 1827. Dr. Frederick Napier practiced here shortly after the Civil War. Dr. J. B. Gatliff, from Williamsburg, Ky., practiced medicine in Mount Pleasant about 1884.

Dr. Noble Smith Howard, who was a licensed practitioner, in 1890 said that before going to Louisville Medical College, he studied under Dr. Gatliff. Dr. "Nobie," as he was called, married Lizzie Howard, daughter of Elhanan Murphy Howard.

There were doctors practicing in the county seat in the 1900's: Dr. Granville Pearl Bailey, who married Margaret Ball; Dr. Elijah L. Green, who married Cumille Howard; Dr. William Turner Nolan, who married Prescious Cornett. These doctors were licensed practicing physicians.

There were midwives, herb doctors and home-curers, who

149

had learned to make teas, potions and lotions. A woman who was naturally handy with the sick was often referred to as a good doctor.

People did not know about germs in the earlier days, and when they did hear of them, the old folks sort of shook their heads as if seeing were believing. However, they had been taught to wash a wound and scorch clean, flaxen cloths in a hot iron pan to use on a wound. They thought the heat was healing and often used hot water for many aches.

There were no apothecary shops in Harlan County in the early days; in fact there was no need for one. Later as more physicians lived near the county seat, the merchants stocked a supply of bottled and packaged drugs.

My father moved from Tan Yard Hill to Harlan Court House in 1888 and bought the corner at Main and Central which is now occupied by a barber shop, jewelry store, beauty shop, and other tenants. He bought this lot for $67.00 and erected a general store. Later he swapped this property for the corner of Central and First diagonally opposite the courthouse which is now occupied by the Green-Mill. He carried a supply of drugs and filled prescriptions according to the doctor's orders. When the Druggist Act passed in Kentucky he became a pharmacist by virtue of his experience in filling prescriptions. Therefore Green-Mill is the oldest drugstore in the town of Harlan. My mother prepared in her kitchen the basic syrups for cough and other liquids and the pills were made up with a base of cornbread crumbs, with the doctor's prescription added.

The care of the babies was a simple matter because the babies were usually healthy and strong. One of the comforts of a large family is that the children had to take turns "minding" the baby while the mother did chores the children could not perform. Most homes had a handmade wooden cradle where the baby stayed during the day but at night the baby usually slept in the same bed with the parents. The most contact the mother had with her infant was at the nursing periods when she sat down with knitting or other hand work and let the baby "suck." It was not considered indelicate

MEDICINE

to expose the breast for baby to nurse when other folks were present because they were so used to it they did not consider it vulgar. Even at church or public gatherings the mothers let the baby nurse openly.

Once in a while a mother would become ill, die or for some reason could not furnish milk to her baby and then a "wet nurse" was employed. Sometimes it was a relative or neighbor who had a young baby and could furnish milk for two and sometimes the "wet nurse" was no relation. My mother once told me of a lady who had not had a child in fifteen years and when her daughter died leaving a newborn baby, the grandmother put the child to her breast and the milk came and she nursed the grandchild whom she "raised" as her own.

The old-timers did not expect to call on a physician for birth or death because that all came just naturally. However they did prepare for both events by getting in a neighbor or relative who was good at taking care of the sick.

Midwifery was practiced to some extent and the pioneers often called a midwife in when there was no relative or neighbor available for "birthing." There was a custom that a sharp hunting knife must be dipped in boiling water before cutting the birthcord. There was another custom that said a new mother must not be moved for three days. Childbed fever was rather common and was probably caused from this old idea that the mother should not be moved. However, I have heard of these pioneers saying that they got up the third day, did all the laundry and took care of the baby. In these old days though it was usually the man who became a widower and remarried.

Everyone wanted and expected to have large families and every birth was celebrated with a feast and this was called a "frolic."

Death was an awesome thing to the pioneer and they took it solemnly and with resignation. A body was never buried the same day of death because there was no way of embalming in those days and the people tried every test they knew to make certain that death was real and not a coma. One test was with a small mirror which was placed in the mouth to try to detect if breath was left. Another one was sticking a pin in the flesh and an experienced person could tell if there was no life in the body.

Pregnancy was accepted as an act of God and the mother-to-be went on with her housework and often worked in the field, besides taking care of the other children. There was no thought of dieting and people would say they must "eat for two." If she craved certain kinds of food every effort was made to get that particular kind of food because they believed the child would be "marked" if the mother had to do without the food she craved.

Children were sometimes born with club feet or hands and many people thought this condition was sent on the parents for some particular sin. I did hear of a farmer whose boy was born club-footed and he tried to do something about it when the child was big enough to walk. He made a wooden splint and whittled it to fit the side of the ankle and foot and tied it with soft deer skin. The people were horrified at what he did as they thought it was very cruel but the boy did grow up with only a slight limp.

One of the ailments which was common in those days was the "grip" and pneumonia, and the little ones often had croup. "Goose grease on a woolen rag" was applied for pneumonia and herbs were given to bring down the fever. Croup was treated with hot melted fat mixed with brewed onion juice and honey and it usually gagged the patient until the phlegm was coughed up.

"Rheumatiz" was treated with hot poultices made of meal, flour and water.

Due to lack of fresh vegetables in the wintertime there was a lot of "summer complaint" when the fresh green things came in spring and when fruit and berries got ripe. This was treated with herb tea and blackberry juice. Some people could tolerate a brew made of parched corn boiled with water, and this furnished nourishment and did not irritate the digestion any more than it was already disturbed. Many babies died with summer complaint and it was an old saying

MEDICINE

that if you could "raise" a baby through the second summer it would live.

Everyone kept remedies on hand at all times and applejack, corn "likker," or peach brandy was an all-cure both for massaging and taking internally. Camphor sticks were placed in a container with whiskey poured over them for rubbing the forehead to relieve headaches. Most fireplaces had a mantel or "farboard" where things like that were kept out of reach of the "younguns."

The pioneer learned to be skillful in setting broken bones, preparing splints and making crutches or canes for the patients.

"Sunstrokes" were quite common in the summertime and they were treated by placing the patient in a prone position in a cool place and applying cool water to their head. Just as often as not, the sunstroke proved fatal and no doubt it was misdiagnosed.

An insect bite of bee, hornet, wasp or bumble bee was treated either by applying whiskey to the sting, a poultice of meal and water or a "chaw" of tobacco laid over the sting area. Snake-bite was treated the same as insect bite except that they made the mistake of drinking the medicine at times.

If anyone got hold of some herb or plant that he thought was poisonous, or ate it by mistake, he was given all the raw eggs and milk he could get down.

If anyone got a fish bone and swallowed it, then he ate a big piece of cornbread to keep the bone from sticking in his gullet.

The bite of any wild animal was considered dangerous, such as rabbit, fox, rat or squirrel, and they used whiskey to rub on it and covered the place with salt. If the wound had not bled any, they usually took a sharp knife and made an "x" on the wound to open it and air it out.

If you stumped your toe, cut it on a rock or jagged stick then a piece of salt pork was placed over the place to draw out the poison.

Chiggers, jiggers or chigoes are little mites which infest

some weeds and there are people who cannot go near them without getting chiggers which burrow under the skin and itch. An application of lard and salt will often relieve the itching and kill the chigger. There is poison ivy or poison vine which is very irritating to some people and then others seem immune. This causes a breaking out and gets hot and feverish where the skin is bothered and itches until you want to scratch and claw at your skin. Meal and water applied to the inflamed parts relieves for a time and then it starts all over again. This keeps up for about a week and the poison ivy has run its course.

Then there are other pests which get on the skin and need doctoring in some manner. There are the little stingin' black gnats that irritate the skin and are bad to get in the eye. When one gets in the eye flax seed is placed on a spoon and the spoon lifted to the eye so that the lid picks up the flax seed and usually gets the sticky gnat out of the eye. The only thing that will get rid of gnats on a sticky, warm night is to keep a fire smoking; the gnat doesn't like smoke.

Everyone got fleas but there wasn't any way to get rid of fleas. You just scratched. Everyone got bedbugs from the wood-logs and you could fight them but you never got rid of them in the old houses.

There were ticks they called wood-ticks which got on dogs, people and cattle. They grew fat sucking blood until they would be as big as the end of the little finger. They had to be picked off dogs and if people got one they pulled it off and applied salt where its head was buried.

There was another kind of tick they called a "wolf" which was an egg or nit that grew into a worm about the size of a chestnut worm or apple worm and where this is buried in the flesh, it festers and has to be squeezed out and salt rubbed on the place.

Every decade or so there have been epidemics in the mountains, not just the children's diseases which everyone thought children had to have, but fevers that really killed grownups.

About the time of the Civil War there was a bad epidemic

MEDICINE

of smallpox. It is thought the soldiers, either on leave or being mustered out, spread it and brought it home with them. I can recall seeing a few people who were pock-marked which leaves horrible scars and fortunately today we see very little of it. There was a man who lived somewhere near Tan Yard Hill who took the smallpox and as soon as he became ill, he recognized the disease from the way folks had described it and he realized that it was contagious. He had no hope of inoculation but he thought of his family and he told them that he was going out to a crib which was about 200 yards from their home and no one was to come near him. He told his wife to make up enough provision to last him ten days and leave it halfway between the house and the crib and he would get it and take it to the crib and stay in the crib. He said that if at the end of ten days, he had not come out, for them to prepare to burn the crib with him in it. He told them not to come near, only close enough for the men to throw pine torches at the crib for it to catch fire and burn up entirely before they came near it. None of the family got the smallpox and everyone thought it was due to his careful preparation to die for them. My father was not sure of the name of the man but he thought his name was Buell. There was a family living near his grandfather within a few miles named Bull and they had their name changed by law to "Buell."

In 1890 there was a bad epidemic of typhoid in the county seat of Mount Pleasant when many people lay sick with fever all summer and several people died. It was a hot, dry spell and the water was low so no doubt the water became contaminated. At any rate several people were sick who did get well and one who got well was my mother.

My mother and father had planned a double wedding on December 25, 1887, with Sallie Bailey and Tyrus Howard when my father took the measles. The other couple got married at Christmastime as planned, but my parents had to postpone their wedding to January 10, 1888. There came a big flood in the river and they were to go to Tan Yard Hill to his people for the infare feast, so when they got to Baxter

FLORENCE HURST BAILEY-BALL
Born 1871—died 1961
Widow of Green Bailey, son of Jonathan K. and Louise Jones Bailey. Her parents were Campbell Hurst and Mary "Pop" Rice Hurst-Kelly. She married Joe Ball, a schoolmaster from Minnesota.

where they had to cross the Cumberland River, the water was very high and dangerous because Poor Fork empties into the river at this junction. Someone "set" them across the river in a flat-bottomed boat and other men had to swim their horses across for them. In the meantime it had turned

MEDICINE

very cold and they had to ride sixteen miles in bitter cold and with the groom just recuperating from measles, it is a wonder they ever lived to tell the tale.

There was an epidemic of typhoid fever in 1890 and Jonathan K. Bailey and his wife Louisa Jones Bailey lost three sons within three months: M. Green Bailey died October 2, 1890; W. R. Bailey died October 13, 1890, and A. J. Bailey died December 21, 1890. M. Green Bailey was married to Florence Hurst and he left her a young widow with two little girls. They had another son Granville Pearl Bailey who became a physician and at this time he was 25 years old, but I do not know if he was practicing at this time. They had two daughters, Sallie who married Tyrus Howard, son of Robert and they had moved to Wasioto; Sudie who married Attorney Green Eversole, son of Rolan who married Lucinda, daughter of Will and Elizabeth Cornett Campbell.

There was an epidemic of meningitis about 1893 that killed several people. There was a couple whose child was desperately ill with this disease and they got down on their knees, imploring Jesus to save their child, and the child lived, but so hopelessly crippled that both parents worked so hard trying to make the child comfortable that they both died young and left him to be a care to someone else.

There was another kind of ailment which a few children had and it was called "fits." It must have been a form of epilepsy, and the pioneers did not know how to deal with this disease. Some even thought it was the devil working inside of the person and they said the patient was "possessed." Fortunately some of the patients outgrew this trouble.

Then there was the type of illness where a child was not "right"; either from a birth injury or congenital causes the child was not mentally able to keep up with the other children. These cases were always taken care of in the homes, and the families tried to give them good attention.

There were people who could not tolerate certain kinds of food but they did not call it allergy. I recall hearing that "Aunt" Cammy Ledford Howard, wife of "Uncle" Henderson Howard, found that she could not eat floured foods, or wheat bread, and she could not eat bread made from cornmeal that had been sifted in the same sifter where flour was sifted. She figured this out by eating certain things one day and then adding another food until she knew that it was wheat flour that disagreed with her. By the same hunt and peck system, people found out which herbs were good for one thing and which ones were good for something else. There was the sassafras tea for thinning the blood in the spring. There was Jimson weed tea for a tonic, and the foxglove was used as a stimulant.

The leech was used to suck blood from a person who thought he had high blood pressure. The leech was a lecherous thing; if you got in the water to wade, fish or frog hunt, a leech would sometimes get on you and have to be pulled off. The people did not know that flies carried germs but they tried to shoo them away and with open doors and no screens there were flies. Frogs liked to catch flies and would often hop right in on the clay kitchen floors and one woman said she called her frog "Rufus."

People had many ways to get rid of warts which they always said were caused from handling toad frogs. Anyway some folks tied a string around the wart real tight and let it stay there for a week when the wart was supposed to drop off. Others said you must rub a greasy dish cloth on it and in a few days it would disappear. To cure a sty on your eye you rub a gold pin or ring on a piece of woolen cloth until it gets hot, place it on the sty and the sty will dry up and go away.

For a boil, or "risin'" as it was called, they took a leaf of the plantain, scorched it and lay it over the boil and it would come to a head. If the tonsils or throat got sore, they made a poultice of clay and water and applied it on the outside of the throat thickly, and let it dry to bring out the soreness.

The pioneers preferred running water for drinking purposes because they thought it was healthier than water that was still; even a spring they wanted to have an outlet and an inlet. They always had their outside toilet which they

MEDICINE

called "privy" below the source of their drinking water.
They were careful to scour their vessels and boiled their clothes in potash lye and sunned and aired their bed clothing whenever possible.

The personal bathing was pretty sketchy when they had to go to the river, branch or else carry water to a wooden tub where they could take a bath. The story was told of a man who came to see his son one day and the little grandson climbed up in his lap but he got right down again and the child's mother said, "Honey, why don't you want to sit on Granpaw's lap?" and the child said, "He stunk lak a bar."

Later the zinc and tin tubs were brought into our mountains which made boiling clothes and personal bathing much easier.

Clyde Gaines' father used to own a place at Cloverport which was built before the Civil War and it had a huge hand-hewn stone tub in it which was a wondrous thing. It had no outlet and when it was filled, the water had to be laboriously bailed and ladled out. We have heard of marble tubs but I once saw a dark metal tub in Chicago which was shipped from England about 1890 and it was thought to be one of the first tubs with plumbing in Chicago. My granpaw lived by a branch which ran along near the house as did most of the mountaineers' homes, and he had a habit of walking barefoot to this branch every night and washing his feet, walking back barefoot before going to bed. Lots of people told him it would kill him to wash his feet in cold weather that way but he lived to be 87 years old although he did suffer from tisic, tiz (asthma).

Then there was the buck fever or buck eager, or buck ague, which old pioneers said was the Indian name for "stage fright." Others said that the white man was so startled when coming face to face with a young Indian brave that the ague resulted and since they often referred to an Indian brave as a buck it may have started from this. Old-timers declared that there was nothing like stalking a bear for days and even though they were prepared, when they met one face to face they often trembled and got so shaky they could not pull a trigger. Anyway buck eager was talked about, joked about and recognized but none of the old-timers ever found a cure for it. They did believe that this quivering, lack of coordination, shaking, quaking, caused by this strange eagerness was a fever anyone might get and God is the only help for it.

In cases of accidents, broken and fractured bones, the treatment and setting of bones was done without anesthetic. They were always glad when a patient was unconscious if any emergency work had to be done because the best they could do was to numb the pain with herb teas.

It was after 1810 that any physician here ever heard of an operation other than simple, minor openings or probing for bullets.

On Christmas day 1809 Jane Todd Crawford agreed to undergo surgery for the removal of a tumor. This was called the "first ovariotomy" and was performed by Dr. Ephriam McDowell at Danville, Ky. She lived some thirty odd years after the successful operation. Weird tales were told by the people who were suspicious of witchery and magic by this doctor who practiced his experiment on ewe sheep in the kitchen of his home. In order not to be disturbed he did this work at night by lamplight and this gave rise to rumors which spread as far as Harlan County and caused people to think he was doing something wrong. It is said that the operation was done on the kitchen table without benefit of anesthesia and after Mrs. Crawford recovered the people's attitude changed because they understood that he was trying to improve his skill.

General George Rogers Clark had a leg removed by a physician in Louisville not too long after the abdominal surgery of Dr. McDowell in Danville. Clark asked that a fife and drum corps march around the building while his operation was being performed which took about two hours. He lived several years after this amputation but he was a tired, "broke" old man, disillusioned because the Commonwealth of Virginia did not reimburse him for his campaigns which he had financed from his own pocket. In 1812 the Virginians

MEDICINE

did grant him a pension and presented him with a sword but he had to go to live with a sister where he remained until his death.

Many of the old pioneers in Harlan had marched with General Clark. Many of them knew him personally, and the Carter and Eager families believe he was related to the two Clark sisters from Wytheville who married John Carter and George Eager and settled on Catron's Creek. They called him Uncle George Rogers and their uncle, who was Henry Clark, used to come to visit them and he spoke of Uncle George Rogers Clark. Their grandfather Christian Seybert went on the Illinois expedition with Clark and received an order for Land Bounty for his trip.

Chapter XIX

RECIPES, RECEIPTS

HOMEMADE remedies and receipts are a part of the heritage of the mountaineer.

Sulphur and lard mixed and applied to skin disease will dry it up.

Dry sulphur sprinkled inside the shoe sole will keep away diseases.

Sulphur and molasses thoroughly mixed and taken as a spring tonic will clear up the complexion and blood.

If you belch at the table you have eaten too much.

If you touch poison ivy, wash in strong home-made lye soap.

Never handle an egg with greasy hands or salty hands or it won't hatch.

The plant called heartleaf makes a good salve for sores.

Bee sting will cure rheumatism.

Tobacco quid will draw out poison of sting when applied.

For poison ivy rub the juice of the succulent wild touch-me-not on the exposed parts.

A few drops of turpentine in a spoonful of water will cure the bellyache.

For bellyache rub dry flour lightly on the abdomen.

A poultice of flour and water is good for mosquito bite.

Goose grease rubbed on the chest, covered with flannel rag will break up congestion.

Cucumber juice will bleach freckles.

To keep the hands white and soft use cucumber juice and sweet cream.

To brush teeth, make a small brush from birch limb and apply salt.

For chapped hands rub with tallow.

Gunpowder tea was used for cramp colic.

Warm tobacco smoke blown into the ear was good for earache.

RECIPES, RECEIPTS

Chew tobacco for toothache.
Chew whole cloves for toothache.
A chew or quid of tobacco applied to a wound will draw out the soreness.
A piece of fat bacon laid on the wound caused by rusty nail will draw out infection.
A poultice of meal and water will bring down swelling or inflammation.
For nose bleed, place cold steel on the spine at base of neck, wet a piece of cloth and place on head.
Drink pepper in whiskey for cold.
For high blood pressure, they punctured a vein and bled the patient.
Tansy tea was taken internally for tiz (asthma).
Foxglove tea was given for heart trouble in small doses as it was very poisonous.
Cucumber juice and cow cream will soothe sunburn.
Butter and honey tied in tiny bag for baby to suck will make baby sleep.
Ivy root boiled down to thick fluid and mixed with lard applied for skin disease. Said to be Indian remedy.
Beech bark tea is taken for dysentery.
Blackberry root boiled for summer complaint.
Red sassafras tea is a spring tonic.
Ivy root tea and tallow applied for itch.
Indian remedy—take the root of the laurel and boil in water until thick, apply for itch, skin disease, poison oak or poison ivy. When the skin begins to burn, then rub with lard to relieve burning.
Blackberry cordial will check diarrhea.
To bring a boil to a head, scorch a plantain leaf and apply to boil while hot and cover with clean cloth.
For fire or grease burn, melt tallow and when cool enough apply to burn with old, soft, clean cloth very lightly.
For burns pour mint tea, that has boiled and cooled, over the burned area.
To improve the complexion, pat with thick buttermilk and let dry.

Beat roots of the slippery elm and make a poultice to pack on a boil to bring it to a head.

Gargle with salt water for sore throat.

Take a spoonful of honey for coughing.

Boil tender poke shoots for delicate stomach.

For headache, place cool pawpaw leaves on forehead and temples.

A boil or "risin' " is worth $5.00 for purifying blood.

A mixture of coal-oil, turpentine and melted lard makes a person vomit if he has eaten or taken poison.

A lotion made from the buckeye sap was used by the Indians for healing skin eruptions, but taken internally was poisonous.

Cockle-burr milk was taken internally for snake bite. You take the whole plant, root and all, wash and boil into a thick liquid, strain and mix with milk.

Acorn nut tea was good for a tonic. The nut was roasted or parched in cinders, then boiled which made a strong tea.

Black walnut juice rubbed on gray hair would give it color. The juice came from the outer husk of the walnut before it dried out.

Black walnut juice was also used for dyeing cloth.

Boiled oak bark also made dye.

Madras was used for dye.

Pig birds are made by stripping the tenderloin from the back bones. Slice small pieces of tenderloin, season and spread with a stuffing made from bread crumbs, roll the meat together and fasten with small skewer, brown in grease, then cover with a lid to simmer for an hour on a slow fire. Gravy can be made in the juice from the "birds."

A pork turkey is made by taking a roll of ribs, spreading with bread stuffing, roll together and fasten with skewer and cook as you would roast turkey.

Sausage is made from trimmings of the shoulder and tenderloin by pounding, beating, or grinding the meat into bits. Season with salt, spices, sage, honey and red pepper. This can be put in bags to hang up and cure, or the sausage can be cooked and placed in a crock and covered with grease to

RECIPES, RECEIPTS

seal it and this will keep until spring. The grease will get rancid but can be used for home-made soap.

Chittlin's are cooked very much like the egg-bag of a hen and were considered a prize dish as were the lights, pancreas, liver and jowl.

To cook an old cured ham, trim off fat, cut off the hock end and save for cooking with vegetables. Soak the ham in cold water in a vessel large enough for water to cover the ham, overnight. Pour off this water and boil in a container with enough water to reach one-third of the ham and put a lid on it. Cook twenty minutes to every pound of ham and when tender, remove vessel from fire and place it out of danger or reach of children and yet the ham cool in the vessel and juice it was cooked in. When cool enough to bear your hand to the vessel, remove the ham to a baking griddle. Spread the ham with molasses, sprinkle with flour and meal to hold in the juices and brown lightly. Cloves and spices may be added, if desired. When cool the ham is ready to slice.

Souse meal is made by boiling the pig knuckles, feet, head and tail together until tender. Remove bones and pour the mixture into a vessel to mold and when cool the gelatin in the juice will keep it firm enough to slice. It can be served cold or the slices can be rolled in meal or flour and fried.

Most of these bread receipts do not call for salt but our family liked to add a little salt. This receipt is said to have been given to the early white settlers by friendly Indians:

SCALDED HOECAKES

Put two cupsful of pounded meal, unsifted, in a vessel and pour boiling water over it, stirring rapidly until smooth and a little thicker than cake batter. Dip your hands in clean, cold water and shape into flat patties and brown on both sides on hot hoecake iron griddle which has been greased generously with bacon drippings which should be smoking hot. Serve with ham and red-eye gravy and vegetables or butter and serve with molasses, honey or maple syrup. I prefer a little salt in my batter but the original recipe did not call for salt.

CORNPONE or HOBBY BREAD

Place two cups meal in vessel, add 1 cupful of buttermilk and one-half teaspoon of soda (the old recipe did not use soda). Mix together with hands or wooden spoon. Thin with cold water until the dough is easy to roll into a ball, then shape in oval patties which we called hobbies and cook in hot iron griddle or skillet which has been well greased. Cook in hot oven or coals about a half hour, depending on the thickness of your pone. (Women usually kept back a spoonful of the dough in a small covered dish to leaven the cornbread for the next day.)

CORN DODGERS

The meal dough is made exactly as Cornpone except that the pones are made into smaller balls and flattened a little to have more crust.

CRACKLIN' BREAD OR SHORTENIN' BREAD

Take three cupsful ground meal, one pint water and one cupful cracklin's. Mix all into a stiff dough, adding a little water if necessary. Bake in heated iron baking pot for about one hour and serve while hot. Cracklin's are the result of rendered fats which leave small brown cracklin's in the bottom of the kettle. The lard is strained through cheesecloth into containers and the cracklin's remain in the cloth bag to be used for shortenin' bread (we prefer to add a little salt).

CORN MEAL MUSH

This is said to be another Indian recipe. Have boiling water in a large iron kettle and gradually add corn meal stirring to keep from forming lumps and keep stirring until the mush is thick and has boiled for a few minutes. Serve with butter and short or long sweetening. I doubt if there is any leftover mush but if there is it can be sliced, rolled in flour and fried in hot grease for another meal.

GRITTED OR ROSENYEAR BREAD

This bread is made in the fall when the roasting ear is too hard for corn-on-the-cob and too green to shell for ground meal. The corn is grated on an improvised gritter, but a good strong cheese grater would do. Grit five or six "years" of corn until you have about three cupsful. The juice in the kernel of the corn should make the gritted meal moist enough without adding water, but if the dough seems too stiff a little water or milk may be added. Pour into a greased smoking hot iron baker and place the heated lid on the baker and heap hot coals on the lid, placing the baker on hot hearth stones and not directly on the red coals. This takes about thirty minutes to brown and should be done all the way through but if the dough is stiff, allow the baker to remain on the hot stone a few minutes longer.

SKILLET BREAD

Place two cupsful of unsifted meal in a vessel and moisten with enough cold water to mix with hands. Now pour bread into a smoking greased iron skillet and place on hot hearthstone near red ashes, keeping covered with iron lid. Remove the lid, allow steam to escape and with a knife or fork raise up the bottom crust to see if it is browned. Take a plate the size of the skillet, place over the top of the skillet, turn the bread into the plate and regrease the skillet, scoot the bread from the plate into the skillet and brown on the other side. The bread should be crusty and brown on both sides and the bread should be done by the time both sides are browned. However if the bread is very thick, allow a little more time for the middle inside to get thoroughly cooked.

SALTRISING OR SALTRISEN BREAD

Cook one Irish potato until tender, mash in water it is cooked in, add 1 cup cornmeal, 1 teaspoon salt, and 1 cup lukewarm sweet milk. Cover and keep in a warm place overnight. Next morning add large tablespoon of soft butter or lard and add one cupful warm water and add flour to make a stiff dough. Set in a vessel of warm water to rise, keeping the water warm. This mixture should rise and when risen, knead and place back in the bessel to rise again. Then mold into a loaf and bake in a greased iron pan or skillet about forty to fifty minutes. In the early days there was no white flour so this bread was very dark but it was smooth and tender.

SHORTS BISCUITS

Two cups flour (called shorts, very dark)
1 cup cornmeal
1 cup buttermilk, fresh—not sour
1 teaspoon cream of tartar
½ cup lard (we add pinch of salt)

Mix well and pinch off small ball of dough, place on greased griddle, pat down the balls and bake in moderately hot oven until brown. For ginger biscuits, save back some of dough, add grated ginger and grated maple sugar to flavor.

BUCKWHEAT CAKES

1 cup buckwheat
1 cup cornmeal
1 teaspoon salt
1 teaspoon cream of tartar
1 tablespoon molasses or sorghum
½ cup sweet milk
1 egg whole

Mix all together into good batter adding water to make the right consistency and drop with spoon on hot greased griddle, turn when brown and serve hot.

GINGER BREAD

1 pinch salt

1 cup sorghum
½ cup soft butter
1 cup sweet milk
1 teaspoon cream of tartar
1 whole egg
1 teaspoon ground ginger
1 pinch other spices, ground
3½ cups wheatshorts and corn meal mixed

Mix and pour into hot greased deep skillet, bake slowly for about one hour. Break into pieces and do not slice.

SPOON BREAD
2 cups cornmeal
1½ cups sweet milk
1 teaspoon cream of tartar
1 or 2 whole eggs
large tablespoon soft butter
½ teaspoon salt

Mix well and pour into greased hot iron skillet and bake slowly until firm. Spoon out while still warm and serve.

Chapter XX

SUPERSTITIOUS SAYINGS

DUE to the various countries from which the early pioneers came, there resulted various superstitions which some firmly believed in and others spoke with their "tongue in their cheek."

There were many bad luck omens, forebodings and forecasting of perilous times, but usually the bad luck could be forestalled by some simple act.

A rooster crowing in the back yard was a sign of death, but if you get up and tell him to go away the spell is broken. If a bird flew in the house it was a sign of death, but if you could shoo the bird out of the house the sign of death was erased.

If your cornbread burns your husband is very angry, and if it scorches, he is out of humor so it is well to be particularly nice to him.

If corn is planted in the rise of the moon it will be barren.

When you hear the call of the rain crow it is the sign of rain.

When you hear a tree frog he forecasts rain.

If you hear a frog in the pond early in spring he will soon see ice.

To take wood into the mountain was like carrying coals to Newcastle.

If you give someone a pin, he must first stick it in wood, or it will bring a split between you.

Never thank a person for giving you a start of seeds or plants or you will have bad luck with them.

Always plant flax on Good Friday.

Stick beans should be planted on Good Friday.

If you put your garment on wrong side out, don't change it or you will have bad luck.

If you dream of muddy water it is bad luck but if you get up and drink clear water it breaks the jinx.

SUPERSTITIOUS SAYINGS

Dream of a death is the sign of a birth.

When an old member of the family dies, there will be a birth to replace this member.

Dream of a birth is the sign of a death, but if you wait until after breakfast to tell it, the sign is broken.

It is bad luck to dream of a wedding unless you hear of an approaching marriage.

Plant a cedar tree and you will die when it is large enough to shade your grave.

A screech owl call is bad luck unless you break a switch and toss it in the fire.

If your right eye itches, you will cry if you rub it.

If your left eye itches, watch out for good news.

If your right palm itches, you will shake hands with a stranger.

If your left palm itches, you will receive money.

If your bones ache it is the sign of falling weather.

If smoke curls to the ground, it is the sign of falling weather.

If the weather clears during the night, the fair weather will not last long.

If the weather is clear at new moon, it is likely to be fair until the moon wanes.

Rain at the change of the moon will last until the change of the moon.

Rain before morning seven, clear before eleven.

A salmon sky is the sign of good weather.

A mackerel sky is one to be doubted.

Thunder in January, frost in May.

When the geese fly over, snow is not far away.

When raindrops remain on the tree, the rain is not over.

Large drops of rain denote a quick storm.

Large drops of rain often bring hail.

Threatening clouds oft go around.

When all the food is eaten on the table, it will be a dry day tomorrow.

For beauty, arise on May Day at daybreak and wash in the early dew.

For beauty arise on May Day and rub the juice of a May apple on the skin.

Some of the sayings and expressions of the mountaineer are unique:

We'uns want ye'uns to come and bring the younguns.
Bettern a mess of sallit (wild salad greens).
It won't do no good.
Don't never do that again.
There hain't been nobody here.
That thar's a long way to borry far (fire).
Fractious as a moony horse.
Ill as a hornet.
You never know a person till you've slept with him.
Touch your black spot and you'll go abroad.
A rolling stone gathers no moss.
A widow "settin' out."
Of a young widow 'tis said, "Rip little Rosie the bridle's loose."
A well-filled table is enough to "feed a log rollin'."
One is dressed up like he is going to an Infair (wedding feast).
Butterm while they're hot (biscuits).
He's just possumin' (pretending sleep).
Take to the woods (hide).
Forninst the hill (over against the hill).
Don't take their sass (impudence).
As treacherous as quicksand.
Don't look for a needle in a haystack.
"Blue john" was skimmed milk.
As stubborn as a mule.
As nervous as a cat.
As plump as a "pattridge."
As pretty as a speckled pup.
As wild as a buck.
As spotted as a pided cow.
As mean as a bay steer.
Light and look at your saddle.
I'd give my eye tooth for it.

SUPERSTITIOUS SAYINGS

As wise as a feller cuttin' his wisdom teeth.
No more sense than a goose.
She makes more noise than a guinea-hen.
Pot can't call the kettle black.
Some things, the more you stir, the more it stinks.
Take care of yourself during dog days.
You can't tell by lookin' at a frog how far he'll jump.
Fine as frog hair.
If you make your bed, sleep in it.
As blind as a bat.
As drunk as a hoot owl.
Each feller's crow is the blackest.
As lanky as a rail.
As mean as the old Scratch.
You can't shovel dirt without getting dirty.
As white as the driven snow.
You can lead a horse to water but you can't make him drink.
As slow as molasses.
As long as the 7 year each (itch).
A darn is more righteous than a tear.
It's the still sow that gets the slop.
A chip off the old block.
Willful waste makes woeful want.
A wasteful wife can throw more out with a spoon than her husband can bring in with a spade.
When poverty comes in the door, love flies out the window.
Chickens come home to roost.
Every family has a skeleton in their closet.
Dead men tell no tales.
Two can keep a secret if one is dead.
Molasses draws flies.
Feed your man honey not vinegar.
When you build a fire it will burn if your lover is true.
A good fire maker has Indian blood in him.
If you are the last of your crowd to get married, you are dancing in a hog trough.

There are more ways of killing a sow than choking it on butter.

Fish will bite before rain.

Keep your counsel until asked for.

Familiarity breeds contempt.

They are as thick as two in a bed.

She is so good butter won't melt in her mouth.

Better be clever than pretty (clever means generous).

She's set her cap for him.

Keep an article 7 years and you will find a use for it.

Pretty is as pretty does.

Beauty is only skin deep.

Still water runs deep.

Do me a favor and I'll dance at your wedding.

You can't trust him as far as you can throw a bull by the tail.

Beware of a sheep killing dog.

A drinking woman is like a horse with the blind staggers.

The steel of a young blade is not yet tempered.

Give a man an honest day's work.

As the tree leans so does the sapling.

Sheep clouds can become dark storms.

Split wood for a rainy day.

Two heads are better than one, even if one is a sheephead.

Many hands make light work.

Too many cooks spoil the stew.

Don't buy a pig in a poke.

Rain will let up in time to milk the cows.

The tomato was called Love Apple and was considered poison or at least unfit to eat until about 1850. They were also called Tommy Toes.

The woodchuck hibernated and in the spring he would often come out in the sunshine and if a cold spell followed he went back into his hole and this gave rise to the saying that if the groundhog sees his shadow there will be six more weeks of winter. I believe the date now is considered February 2.

SUPERSTITIOUS SAYINGS

When a horse shies and is skittish it is the sign he senses danger near.
It is good luck to hear the Bob White call.
The squeaky wheel gets the grease.
A "hawse pistol" is a rapid fellow.
Straight as an arrow.
As clean as a hound's tooth.
Rotten to the bone.
As slick as slippery elm.
As cool as a cucumber.
A new broom sweeps clean.
When Cornwallis surrendered his sword to General Washington, one of our old soldiers was there and he told that Cornwallis said, "Cornwallis is taken, root hawg, or die" and so the expression root hog, or die is still used in the mountains.

  Monday's child is wise tho slow
  Tuesday's child has far to go
  Wednesday's child is full of woe
  Thursday's child works hard for a living
  Friday's child is loving and giving
  Saturday's child must beware
  Sunday's child is very fair.

  Marry in red you wish yourself dead
  Marry in black you want to go back
  Marry in blue you'll always be true
  Marry in white you should be alright
  Marry in green you want to be seen
  Marry in yellow, watch your fellow
  Marry in gray you go far away.

A beeswarm in May is worth a stack of hay.
A beeswarm in June is worth a silver spoon.
A beeswarm in July is worth not a fly.
It is lucky to carry a buckeye with you.
It brings good luck for a cat to come to your home.

A black cat crossing your path is unlucky unless you cross your two forefingers.
If you spill salt, sprinkle some over your left shoulder.
If you turn over a chair, you won't get married this year.
Don't count your chickens afore they hatch.
It is bad luck to step on a grave.
You are liable to have bad luck if you go through a graveyard at night.
See granddaddy long legs, make a wish.
Don't look at a new moon through brush.

Ollie Cornett Lewis (Mrs. W. W. Lewis), Lucy Brittain Howard (Mrs. M. R. Howard). These daring young women are wetting their feet in Clover Fork.

SUPERSTITIOUS SAYINGS

It is lucky to see a new moon with no trees obstructing your view.

If your nose itches, you will soon see a stranger.

If you drop your dishcloth, company is coming for dinner.

You dig your grave with your teeth.

If you lose a tooth, place it under your pillow and it will turn to a silver spoon.

The dog tooth or eye tooth gives you strength.

Your last teeth or wisdom teeth will give you knowledge.

If you sleep in a strange room, name the corners and you will marry the one you face when you awaken.

Two forks or two knives at one place setting is bad luck when the setting calls for only one.

Thank someone for a plant, it will not thrive.

Don't give scissors for a gift unless they give you a penny.

When two people walk along, and a post or tree separate you, say "bread and butter" or it will cut your love in two.

A child will be birthmarked if the mother-to-be cannot have the food she craves.

If a person gets his foot wet in Clover Fork he will always return to Harlan County.

It is lucky for a bride to marry in white.

It is lucky for the sun to shine on your wedding day.

Never start a job on Friday, you may not finish it.

If a sickly person can make it through the falling leaves he will live to see them fall again.

If an acquaintance fails to recognize you there will be a wedding soon.

If you spit on your bait the fish will bite.

If you spit on your bait and name it, your lover likes you if you catch a fish.

If the palm of your foot itches, you will go abroad.

Never start a journey on Friday.

If you meet a hay wagon, make a wish and it will come true.

If you see a hay wagon it is good luck.

If you see a falling star, make a wish and it will come true.

The first star you see at dusk repeat this saying: "Star light, star bright, I wish I may, I wish I might have this wish I wish tonight," and it will come true.

April borrowed ten days from March to kill old cows with.

Red light at night shepherd's delight, red light in the morning, sailor's warning.

Plant potatoes in the dark of the moon.

Kill hogs on the wane of the moon. If you kill hogs on the rise of the moon you will not render any lard fat.

If the new moon is misty, it is full of water.

When birds wallow in dirt, it is sign of rain.

If it rains the first Sunday of the month, each succeeding Sunday will be rainy for four weeks.

A blue bird or red bird in winter means snow.

When the robin comes it is the sign of spring.

If it rains while the sun is shining, it will rain at that time on the morrow.

Chapter XXI

PASTIMES

IN THE wintertime the weather was often too bad for the men to hunt, clear new ground, split rails, or cut down trees. The days were short so the meals were prepared by daylight as much as possible. The men usually took care of the stock and cattle and fed the chickens in bad weather so they had long hours to pass by the fireside. This meant, too, that the children were more or less penned indoors so they thought up pastimes to keep them occupied. There were indoor games the whole family took part in like drawing on slates, whittling and playing guessing games. These guessing games were really educational although they did not think of them as "larnin'." One member would start the guess by naming a well-known person like Benjamin Franklin and others would join in by naming every notable they had heard of and when this subject was exhausted they went on to naming States, Rivers, Streams and so on. If the schoolmaster happened to be boarding with the family at the time, he was a great addition to their game. Other games were trees, plants and shrubs with which they were all familiar and sometimes they would group plants into subjects like name a color which could be Bluebell, yellow root, red bud, cherry blossom, white clover, indigo and many others. Then they would start naming plants with animals in the name such as dogwood, catnip, crabapple, goat sour, fox grape, toad stool, flea bane, turtle root and so on. Then they would take the subject of a name mentioned in a flower such as Jimson weed, Queen Anne's lace, Johnny-jump-up, Reed, sweet William, Rose, Daisy, Violet and so on. Plants which have the name of some member of the body would be another game like heartleaf, bladder wort, boneset tea, bears foot, horseheal, buckeye, sow's ear, louse wart, maiden hair, skull cap, beard tongue, chestnut, shin leaf and mouse ear. Clothes or accessories made another subject like hemlock, fir, pokeberry, dutchman britches, sumac, rag weed, skull cap, umbrella fern, fox glove. There was the season and time of day mentioned in plants like Fairmaid of February, Juniper, Mistletoe, May apple, morning glory, spring beauty, star flower, sunflower, snow drop, summer fern, winter fearin, dewberry, thyme, windflower, swampweed and so on. Names of farm life appearing in plant names like buttercup, hen and chickens, iron weed, sawbriar, bellflower and Indian paint brush. Birds added another game like what bird mimics—answer mocking bird; corn thief is a crow; a Kentucky color—cardinal; high nest—eagle; plackity-plack—guineas; meow-meow bird—catbird.

The custom of reciting psalms and passages from the Bible was popular and hymn singing was something that all joined in. Any kind of musical instrument was used and encouraged by each member of the family.

Outings outside the house took place during good weather when the crops did not press too heavily and the whole countryside attended funerals, weddings, infair feasts, baptizings and preachings. A meeting at the church was an all-day affair and the women prepared great baskets of food to spread on the ground which everyone was welcome to eat. There were singing meets, spelling bees, fiddling contests, square dances where anyone could get up and solo with a buckwing, or jig. The Kentucky Running Step was a favorite with everyone as was the Virginia Reel. The caller was an important addition to singsonging the calls which most of the folks knew by heart.

In the fall of the year, picnics were planned when couples went "a-nuttin' " and they brought back sacks of chestnuts and other edible nuts. Pawpaw picking was another outing as was a persimmon hunt. Berry picking was joined in by whole families. Quilting bees were left to the women folks while log raisings were the men's work.

Hog killing time was a busy day for all the family. In the first place the men had to go hunting to get their hogs for they were not usually kept penned up and several neighbors took part. All the family worked at it and each did their part in sharing the work and dividing the meat. One of the first things the householder had to build was a meat house which had a clay sod floor so that a hickory fire could be made of green wood to smoke and cure the hams, bacon and sausage. Then the rafters had to be high enough to string the meat away from rats and the smoke helped to keep away insects. Of course it took a heavy door to keep away "varmints." A big iron pot was placed on a fire outside filled with water which was kept boiling to clean the hog, and this was a danger about children getting hurt. Then there were the hungry dogs looking for a handout because the early settler needed several kinds of dogs for different kinds of hunting and watchcare. When the meat was all trimmed and ready, then sausage meat had to be ground or pounded into bits and placed in a large vessel to season with sage, salt, spices, pepper and honey. Red hot pepper was one of the garden vegetables that was used freely by the women in their cooking. It was considered healthy and was even put in chicken feed in the wintertime to perk up their health.

We knew a girl who had been away to a school at Lexington and in those days a vacation leave was Christmas and sometimes at Easter. Travel connections were not as convenient as nowadays so that a student would not have time to make the return trip for the week-end or half-week. However, this girl got an unexpected few days and she decided to surprise her mother and not tell her that she was coming home. Every other time when she came home, her mother had prepared chicken and dumplings and other good "company" dinner, but this particular Saturday that she came home, she walked into the kitchen and it was full of sausage meat to be made up. At hog-killing time, the kitchen is in such a mess that the supper meal is necessarily light because the kitchen is taken up with the meat. Our girl friend said that cured her from ever surprising anyone again.

Coney stew (rabbit) and squirrel meat was considered a good dish by the early settlers and when they could find no other game, a rabbit was usually to be found. They are garden robbers anyway because they like the vegetables the farmer raises. While the rabbit is quick and swift, he is much easier to catch than the squirrel which is so nimble and quick that a person can hardly hit one. Too, a different kind of gun has to be used on the squirrel and rabbit. Because of tearing up the meat, it takes a lightweight gun while hogs, bears, buffalo and buck were usually hunted with a "hogrifle." Wild turkey and fowls and birds were also hunted with a lightweight gun although some men could get them with a slingshot.

Boys and men did the hunting for the families as well as fishing which furnished most of the meats for the early settlers. Younger boys played jack-knife by pitching an open-bladed knife on a log and they would practice this for hours. Pebble throwing and using the slingshot engaged young boys by the hours. John Blanton Lewis who was raised at Four Mile became so quick and skillful with a pebble that he could bring down a bird on the wing. They practiced using the sling shot to bring down squirrels which were so nimble that it took a quick eye to hit one.

Then there was a contest of skill usually held once or twice a year on the "greens" or "commons" which would be a level open field. Boys engaged in running races and young men held a contest to prove the prowess in the joust game. The combatants used a trimmed branch, longer than a walking cane and not as heavy as a club, with a rounded, smooth end. Working on foot, something like fencing, each tried to keep the other fellow from touching him with the jousting pole. When one of the contestants touched the other fellow, the game was over and the toucher was the winner.

There were horse races which were held in fields that were used as race tracks and usually there were some game rooster "fiats" on the side. The hardy pioneers were not above wagering on these pastimes.

Then there was the game of horseshoe pitching (or quoits) which the men enjoyed especially when they bested the other fellow.

There were a few games which the girls and boys could enjoy together such as spin the pan, ring around the Rosie

PASTIMES

and dropping the handkerchief. Girls were not allowed to go in the water and few of them learned to swim and most of the boys who learned to swim, sneaked away from home to the nearest swimmin' hole and stripped their clothes off and went in naturally. Occasionally a father could get time to teach his son to swim but usually the boys managed to learn to swim without benefit of instruction, unless an older brother or friend would keep an eye out for him.

Most of the girls learned to ride horses or mules but it was not encouraged because the "critters" were needed for work on the farm.

Fishing made up one of the greatest pastimes for the early settlers. Men and boys did most of it because the women could hardly find time and take all the children, although occasionally the whole family would go a-fishing. They used most anything for bait from worms, crawdads, grampuses, minnows, pieces of fat meat or tallow, and the hook was a crude crooked wire with a homemade line on a pole that had been cut and trimmed. Sometimes the men would go a-gigging which meant they took a sharp gig or stick and by torch light they could spear all the fish they could eat. Frogs were hunted in much the same manner. It seems to me that there has been a law passed some years back where the giggin' is not allowed. Then there was another way they caught fish by using what they called a trotline which was strung from one bank to the other and after a rain when the fish are going downstream they would lodge against the trotline and be caught. This also was outlawed, I believe, because too many fish were wasted in this manner.

In the fall of the year, the old-timers celebrated many ways because their crops were in and fruit and vegetables were plentiful. "Apple Peelin's" was a gathering attended by everyone in the neighborhood. It took a lot of apples to make apple butter which was cooked slowly in a large kettle over an outside fire. Apples burned easily while cooking so a stirrer was wielded by someone constantly while the butter was simmering. The stirrer was a long wooden handle with a wooden hoelike attachment so that one could stand far away enough from the heat and stir to keep the butter from scorching. When the apple butter was done, it was flavored with spices and stored in large stone crocks. While the women peeled apples and made the apple butter the men were just as busy making fresh apple cider on a homemade cider press. When the cider was fresh, it was soft cider and when it aged it was called hard cider.

While these activities were going on, someone had to prepare food because there would be many children besides the grownups. Sweet potatoes were roasted in the jackets; "rosenyears" were cooked in the shuck; chicken, ham, or other home-cured meat was cooked in large quantities. Bread was some form of corn-meal bread and while the apple butter was cooking the food was placed where it could be eaten picnic style.

There were other pastimes that were actually work but when the neighbors and families gathered in to help "many hands made light work" and they took pleasure in it. Every family depended on beans in some form for part of their winter diet and so "bean stringin' " became a celebration. The beans were broken up into pieces and dried on rooftops, or the beans were strung with needle and twine and hung over rafters to dry. This method of curing beans was very effective and when the beans were cooked in the winter, they were called hay-beans or shuck-beans.

A "stir-off" came when the cane was cut to grind and press out the sweet juice which had to be boiled down to make sorghum or molasses. This was another occasion when groups got together to make this kind of work a pleasant affair. Somewhere on another fire, apples were roasted, corn grains were parched, chestnuts were boiled in a kettle in their hull and apple cider was nippy at this time in the year because "stir-offs" usually occurred after frost.

CHAPTER XXII

POLITICS, LAWS, COURT PROCEDURES

HARLAN COUNTY has always been dry with the exception of a few years following the repeal of prohibition. Up to that time there seemed to be plenty of "likker," "blind tigers," "moonshining" and "settinhens." At one period in the county the law allowed three legal stills in Harlan County which were for wholesale and not retail consumption. Back in the earliest days a fellow made just what his family needed through the year and to offer to friends who came in and there was no necessity for buying or selling. Corn whiskey was considered the best of the homemade "likkers" but it was also an art to get it perfect. Corn in all forms was probably our most versatile crop which we depended on from the fresh green corn, "rosenyears" baked in the shuck, parched corn snacks, parched corn tea, hominy, bread, and corn for the animals. There were other forms of hard drinks such as apple cider both soft and hard, applejack, peach brandy and "punkin" brandy, grape, berry and persimmon wines.

Harlan County operated under the laws of the Commonwealth of Kentucky. It is my understanding that only three or four states are Commonwealths. The districts were referred to as bailiwicks and a legal sale was a public outcry.

The Justices of the Peace were empowered to perform marriages and in looking up marriage records the letter "Pr" is often noted after the name of the man who officiated at the wedding and he may have been a Justice of the Peace because on the blank to be filled out, I have been told that the letter "Pr" was printed in the form.

Gabriel Slaughter was the governor at the time Harlan County was formed and he appointed Colonel George Brittain to be the Court Clerk which was very fitting because he served in the legislature and was instrumental in helping to have the County of Harlan organized. Richard Balenger was Deputy Clerk. Samuel Howard, Sr., was Coroner and Benjamin Horn, Sheriff. Justices of the Peace were John Noe; William Taylor; Abner Lewis; Elisha Green. These officers took their jobs seriously and showed deference to the law and the court for which they were appointed.

Joseph Eve was Circuit Judge for the 15th District including Harlan, in 1820.

In 1820 Luke Noe was Justice of the Peace.

In 1820 Ephriam Osborn and wife Polly signed a deed.

In 1820 John Noe made a deed to James Dixon.

In 1820 John Lewis made a deed to Ephriam Sergeant.

In 1820 Elisha and Nancy Green made a deed to Jesse Cope.

In 1820 George and Nancy Hoskins made a deed to John Bingham.

In 1821 Wilson Lewis had John Lewis invested with power-of-attorney for the estate of Wilson Lewis, deceased, late of Knox County.

In 1820 John B. Blanton deed to Gabriel Jones.

In 1821 Mathias Kelley deed to John Pennington.

In 1821 Samuel Mark deed to George Osborn.

In 1822 Patrick Napier deed to William Napier.

In 1822 John Gas deed to Henry and Hezekiah Branson.

In 1823 Solomon and Polly Burkhart deed to George Coldiron.

In 1823 Samuel Ewing deed to Moses Ball.

In 1824 Jesse Brock, Sr., deed to Aaron Brock.

In 1824 Court appointed Squires:

Samuel Howard	John Jones
John Creech	William Green
Hiram Jones	Elisha Green
Jonathan Kelley	Lewis Green
Joseph Benjey	Solomon Taylor
John Hendrixon	

In 1824 Henry Smith bought land from John Harrison on Poor Fork.

POLITICS, LAWS, COURT PROCEDURES

In 1825 Benjamin Osborne made deed to John Harris, Clover Fork.

In 1825 Berry Cawood made deed to John Cawood.

In 1825 Zachariah Jones bought land from George Brittain on Clover Fork.

In 1826 Henry Shackleford bought land from William Spurlock on Martin's Fork.

In 1828 William Taylor was County Judge, his wife's name Catherine.

Aug. 5, 1826, Stephen Farmer made deed on Martin's Fork to John Farmer stating John is his youngest son and excepted land already acquired by Lewis Farmer.

In Jan. 1828 Stephen S. Jones made power-of-attorney to Richard Wilburn.

In 1826 Thomas and Betsy Hoskins made deed to Hiram Hoskins on Browney's Creek.

In 1830 Robert Deprest bought land from John Farmer on Straight Creek.

From 1828 to 1837, John Gilbert was State Senator representing Clay, Knox, Harlan and Whitley Counties. He had been a Revolutionary soldier and was forefather of Judge James M. Gilbert who served this district as Circuit Judge in the thirties.

In 1830 John Dixon was Justice of the Peace.

In 1831 John and Sally Spicer made deed to John Hoskins, witness Robert George, Yellow Creek (now Middlesboro).

In 1831 Henry Tuggle was Clerk of the Harlan County Court.

In 1832 Col. Elijah Green was Justice of the Peace.

In 1834 John Crump was Justice of the Peace.

In 1834 Joseph Eversole was Judge of the Harlan Circuit Court.

In 1833 John Hoskins made deed to Thomas Hoskins for North's Improvement—witness Hiram Hoskins.

1833 Justices of the Peace appointed:

Luke Noe   Jonathan Kelly
John Creech   Bailis Shumate

In 1833 Thomas Hoskins made deed to Hiram Hoskins—Hoskins Ford.

1832 Mount Pursiful and Robert George were Justices of the Peace.

1832 Robert George made deed to Jess Durham on Straight Creek.

1836 Moses B. Evans was Justice of the Peace.

1839 Jack (John) McGeorge was Sheriff of Harlan Co., 32 years old.

In 1839 Isham Jones was Justice of the Peace.

In 1840 John Dixon was Justice of the Peace.

In 1842 John Lewis was Justice of the Peace.

In 1845 Jonathan Smith was County Surveyor.

In 1846 Hiram Lewis was Justice of the Peace.

In 1850 David Turner was Justice of the Peace.

In 1850 John Lewis was County Judge, 29 years of age.

In 1853 Mose Cawood was Justice of the Peace.

In 1857 William Middleton was Justice of the Peace.

In 1860 C. B. Brittain was U. S. Marshall.

In 1865 John Farmer was Justice of the Peace.

In 1867 T. H. Noe and Hiram C. Lewis were Justices of the Peace.

In 1868 Elijah Hurst was Justice of the Peace.

In 1870 John Robert Rice was appointed Assistant Town Marshall of Mount Pleasant.

In 1870 Judge W. C. L. Huff served as County Court Clerk. Later he was made County Judge and City Judge. He was born 1846 and died in 1939 at age of 93.

In 1874 Lewis Farmer was Clerk, Harlan County Court.

In 1877 S. C. Huff was County Court Clerk.

In 1882 William F. Hall was a young barrister in Harlan.

In 1888 Green A. Eversole was a young barrister in Harlan.

In 1890 Wilson Lewis was Harlan County Judge.

In 1890 B. F. Nolan was elected Superintendent of the Common Schools.

In 1890 William Lankfort was appointed Town Marshall of Mount Pleasant.

POLITICS, LAWS, COURT PROCEDURES

In 1892 Henry L. Howard was appointed Commonwealth Attorney for Harlan County.

At the turn of the century John Ance Ward was Sheriff and William L. Bailey was County Judge in 1900.

Taxes were paid to the county seat and the old records are at the old Capitol Building in Frankfort. Among some of the 1820 old tax receipts were:

William Griffith on Poor Fork, 75 acres at $1.00 per acre.

John Back, Poor Fork, Hezekiah Branson and Noble Blair.

Moses Ball and Bennet Ball on Catron's Creek.

Carr Brittain and Solomon Burkhart on Martin's Fork.

Jesse Brock, Sr., 206 acres on Cumberland River, $5.00 per acre.

William Blanton, Wallins Creek, 200 acres.

Galvin Bailey, Nimrod, Andrews, Car and Vincen—Clover Fork.

Thomas Ball on Clover Fork.

John, Joshua, and William Bingham, Browney's Creek.

Joseph Bengeny, Cumberland River.

Bounty was paid for "varmints"—Eagle $7.00, Wolf $6.00, Bear $5.00, Panter $3.00, Weasel & Fox $2.00, groundhog $1.00. The skins were brought into the courthouse at a regular term of court and the warrants allowed for the clerk to issue. "APRIL TERM OF COURT 1841

Commonwealth

Moses Wilder Wolf .... $ 6.00
John Gilliam Wolf 6.00
David Maggard Wolf 6.00
David Gillam & Samuel Creech 36.00
David Maggard, Wolf 36.00
Wm. Boggs Wolf 6.00

"AT A COURT HELD IN HARLAN, October 1839 John Crump, Clerk of the Court, returned that he had received $33.25 as tax on deeds, county seals, horses, etc., and no more since May 1st to present term of Court, which sum

189

Courtesy of the Harlan Daily Enterprise
Judge J. Grant Forester, son of Lieut John W. Forester and Nancy Howard Forester. He married Jane Hall-Blackburn, a widow, daughter of Nathan and Louise Brittain Hall.

after making 5 per cent compensation he is ordered to pay balance to Trustee of the Jury Fund, signed Joseph Eve, Judge.

John Fee claim .... .50
John C. Howard claim 5.12½
Wm. Wright claim 5.74
John G. Crump, Clerk for minute book 5.87½
Clerk ex-officio 40.00

POLITICS, LAWS, COURT PROCEDURES

Thomas Sewell, jail claim 11.42
George Crider 2.10
John McGeorge, Constab. 5.00
Trustee of Jury Fund 26.15
Thomas Sewell, guard 19.90
William Turner, Jr. 19.90

"Verdict: We, the Jury, find the defendant guilty of charge contained in indictment and we further agree and find that he should receive five lashes at the public whipping post for said county on his bare back. Signed John Gillam, one of the jury. Jurors: Moses Ball, Henry Skidmore, Anthony Saylor, William Ledford, William Dixon, Wright Bailey, Luke Jones, John Gillam, Jepe Bailey, John Maggard, Ed Crump and George Blanton."

Harlan County Court 1841
We the Jury, find for the plaintiff against each defendant $3.75 for damage. signed
William Green, one of the Jury.
Jurors: Anthony Saylor, Jerry- Brewer, Edmund Gross, Wright Bailey, George Blanton, Elias Arnett, John Smith, James Seargent, John J. Howard, David Smith, John Gillam, William Green.
John G. Crump, claim, ex-officio services from October 1939 and October 1840, $40; William Collins, wolf certified $36; William Smith, wolf certified $18; William D. Green, for comparing polls $10.25.

APRIL TERM 1854.
Claims allowed: William Blanton, guard .75 for Commonwealth; William Blanton, wildcat killed $1; John Barnett, wildcat $1; William Brok, $1 wildcat killed; Joseph Blair, wildcat $3; John Cawood, wildcat $1; James Howard, wildcat $1; John Helton, wildcat killed $1; Aley Ledford, wildcat killed $2; Lee Brittain, witness 50¢ for Commonwealth; Walter Middleton, wildcat killed $12 total; James A. Rice, wildcat $1; Stephen Rice, wildcat killed $1; John Rice, wildcat $1; Abram Skidmore, wildcat killed $2; Soloman Saylor, deputy sheriff 80¢.

Representatives from Harlan County in the early days were James Culton, Carlo Brittain, James Farmer, John Jones, James Sparks, Hiram Jones, Elijah Baker, Milt Unthank, Elijah Hurst, William Ward, A. G. W. Pouge, Drury Tye, Robert George, James Lane, Thomas Buford and George Brittain Turner. Senators from Harlan County were Robert George and Franklin Ballinger and T. Jeff Pearcfield.

In 1890 to 1891 the delegate to the Kentucky Constitutional Convention was J. Grant Forester and he was among those men who drafted Kentucky's fourth constitution. He was a fine looking man and was hailed as the silver-tongued orator of the mountains. He had a ready wit and could talk rings around many of his constituents.

SHERIFF GRANT SMITH

POLITICS, LAWS, COURT PROCEDURES

As late as 1890 unclaimed land was being acquired by authorization for anyone who proved the survey and went to the Court for the purpose of appropriating the land.

"May 5, 1890 by George W. Crider, Justice of the Peace, on motion of Dillon Asher, it is ordered and hereby authorized to appropriate 200 acres of the vacant and unappropriated land of Harlan County, he having paid the county price of 5¢ per acre therefor by having same entered and surveyed as required by law. A copy attest, W. C. L. Huff C. H. C.C."

Hiram C. Lewis as of same date in same manner acquired 100 acres.

John Templeton, same date acquired 100 acres.

Ranson Turner July 1890 acquired 100 acres.

Judge Wilson Lewis was Judge of Harlan County in 1890.

F. S. Hensley was jailer 1893 and his wife Elizabeth Lewis was daughter of Eli and Cynthia Lewis.

In the late 1880's A. B. Cornett served as Clerk and County Judge.

Judge John Riddle Sampson of Middlesboro practiced law at the Harlan Court for many years and two of his sons, Will and Ed Sampson, came here to live and later James Sampson came to Harlan to practice law.

Judge Marcellus Moss who married Amanda Bingham held Court in Harlan.

James Campbell, son of Wilkerson Campbell and Martha Perciful Campbell, was representative at Frankfort. Being of a friendly nature, he liked to visit a different church each Sunday. One day he came to his boarding house after church and one of the boarders asked him where he went to church and he told him he attended the Catholic Church. The boarder asked him how he got along and he said, "Fine, I riz when they riz and fell when they fell."

In 1896 a man named Overton was hanged here because he was implicated in the murder of an old couple who peddled through the mountains. It was the stern duty of Sheriff Grant Smith to cut the rope that sprung the trap, October 15, 1896, the day this boy was hanged.

Grant Smith was the son of Jonathan P. Smith and Flora Ann Metcalf Smith who married June 15, 1848, and their certificate was signed by Hiram Lewis. "What God hath joined together let no man put asunder." Matt. XIX, Poor Fork, Ky."

Politics in the eighteen twenties were much more simple than they are today. In the first place the whole population of Harlan County which now includes Bell, parts of Letcher and Leslie was less than two thousand in 1820. Candidates for office made no attempt to see all the voters, they just sent word by a friend and invited them to come to see them when they were in town. Now that was the day of reckoning, when County Court convened the candidate would probably have more guests than there was food to feed them. Primaries were held at the county seat and the candidate was announced while all the interested voters stood around in the courthouse yard or if it rained they went inside. As the candidate was announced the voters took their place in a line and the votes were counted verbally while they stood in their places. In later years near the turn of the century for some reason politics became so hot that primaries could not be held out in the open any longer and the vote had to be taken by ballot. By 1870 the population had increased to 4,415 and by that time Bell County had been taken off Harlan County so that there must have been more people who wanted county offices. Tension became so real during meetings or public speakings that someone would start shooting at the drop of the hat and so the Indian name of Caintuck, meaning dark and bloody ground, was given literally to Harlan and for years it was called "Bloody Harlan."

After the Civil War, Harlan County became predominately Republican although there remained some Democrats here. One old man, S. Critt Howard, was said to have explained it by saying that while Harlan County was divided as to the North and South, the people here did not want to secede and so gradually politics grew hot and hotter. S. Critt Howard was a practicing barrister and had been elected to the office of County Attorney.

POLITICS, LAWS, COURT PROCEDURES

My father remained a Democrat and when I was a little girl, his frends teased me and called me a rebel and I felt that they were trying to belittle me. There was no Democratic Primary for a period of several years that I recall and the Democrats could vote only in national and state elections, because there were not enough Democrats to hold a Primary election.

As politics waxed warmer and hotter, it became necessary more than once to call out the Militia. At the turn of the century the governor's race became so hot that when the election was certified for the Republican candidate William Taylor, the faction for the Democrat William Goebel contested the election and won. As Goebel went down the steps of a public building, he was shot from a window of an office building. Before he died he was sworn in on his deathbed so that the Democrats could hold office. Harlan County became involved because the window where witnesses thought the bullet came from was an elected Secretary of State named Caleb Powers. His brother John L. Powers came to Harlan County to hide out and no one would give away his hiding place. My mother and father were sure that her brother and brother-in-law were hiding him but we do not know to this day, although it is known that John Powers hid in Harlan until he could get out of the country and I understood that he went to South America.

Chapter XXIII

WARS

HARLAN COUNTY has been affected by all wars, being settled largely by Revolutionary scouts who either received land grants or traded with other Revolutionary soldiers. Harlan County was a gateway from the east to the west and the Northwest Territory so that many soldiers and scouts had passed through on their way to Fort Harrod and other stations, thus learning about this area.

During the French and Indian War, Harlan County was raided by bands of outlaw Indians and did not actually see any battles.

The Civil War came to Harlan County because Cumberland Gap was then located partly in Harlan County. The Gap, being a strategic point, was occupied by both the Union and Confederate units who fought to hold this lookout post. Our local boys took part in some of these battles. General Morgan and his men once camped in what is now Georgetown Addition and General Humphrey Marshall with about 3000 southern forces drilled on the field which is now the depot. It is said that at one time 12,000 Yankees marched through here on their way to the South, having routed the Rebels who had forted near Pound Gap.

Following every war in which the United States has been involved, the people have almost invariably elected a soldier-hero to office. George Washington was made president after the Revolutionary War. Andrew Jackson was elected president after the war of 1812. Zachary Taylor was made president following the war with Mexico. After the Civil War, Ulysses Grant was elected president. He was nicknamed "Warhoss." Theodore, "Teddy," Roosevelt was made president following the War of 1898. He is called "Big Stick Teddy" because of his aggressiveness. After World War One John "Jack" Pershing was a popular favorite although he was not made president. Following World War Two, "Ike" Dwight D. Eisenhower was elected president.

It was a common practice for people to name their children after the president or his wife. George Washington was a popular name, as was Andrew Jackson. Zachary and Ulysses were favorite names for children. Following the Spanish-American War, Dewey and David and Theodore were popular names for boys.

This is an incomplete list of the Revolutionary soldiers and patriots who lived in Harlan County:

Carr Bailey, Sr. and wife. Mary Bailey furnished supplies for the Revolutionary Army. They had children: a daughter Betty; James, John, Joseph, Minter and William.

Capt. John A. Bingham married Debora Phipps. James Caudill is buried in Whitesburg Cemetery, born 1749, died 1850.

Robert du Priest (Deprest, dePriest) bought land on Strait Creek. One of his daughters married Josh Bingham.

Capt. Vincen Hobbs, one of the first settlers to live on Catron's Creek at the farm known as the Henry Smith Farm, now owned by Dr. David Hill Smith. It is said that at one time this land changed hands for a rifle which was more valuable than land.

Joseph Hoskins served in the Virginia State Regiment, entered War March 1, 1777. His name appeared on the payroll 1779 for the months December, January, February, March and April, 1780, for the whole amount that was paid "66 dollars and 60/90ths." He received land grant of one hundred acres #3677 in January 1785. His commanding officer was Col. George Gibson.

Jesse Brock, Revolutionary Soldier-Pension 30887 N. Car., born Dec. 8, 1751, moved to Harlan County before 1800, died 1836. He is buried in the Wallins Creek Cemetery. His wife was Rebecca Howard and their daughter Mary married John Coldiron who is buried near Jesse Brock. Their daughter Polly Coldiron married Adron Howard and both are buried nearby.

Joshua Pennington was a scout engaged in expeditions

against the Indians. His sister Jemimah Smith, who was born 1760, stated that he was with Ephriam Osborn in Montgomery Co., Va., under Capt. Enoch Osborne and Lt. James Ward in the U. S. Service.

William Cornett, Revolutionary soldier, is buried in Perry Co. He married Rhoda Gillum, Poor Fork, Harlan County. One of their daughters, Elizabeth, married Will Campbell.

John Gilbert, Revolutionary soldier, was Representative in 1833-1837 including Harlan, Clay, Knox and Whitley counties. He was a Baptist minister for sixty years. He is buried in Clay County on Red Bird River.

Vachel Davis had his application for pension rejected— he applied in 1837. Possibly his service was of short duration.

James Hall, born in Loudon Co., Va., May 10, 1751, drafted in South Carolina, 1776. He lost the use of his right arm. He died in Harlan County July 1837 and had been preaching the gospel for over thirty years. He lived about two miles from Lewis Green, the Revolutionary soldier, near Tan Yard Hill. It is supposed that he preached at the old meetin' house nearby.

Lewis Green, Revolutionary soldier, born 1751 in Virginia, died 1836 in Harlan County and was buried at the old Meetin' House Branch on Tan Yard Hill. Enlisted at Fort Chriswell in 1776 and served 7 years, allowed pension of $40 per year from 1831 until his death. He married Easter or Esther Kilgore.

George Burghart made application for pension in 1831. In Lee County, Va., he stated that he was a resident of Harlan County but lived only about seven miles from the Lee County Courthouse. He said he had lived where there was constant danger from Indian depredations, and served several years as an Indian scout and spy. His son Isaac Burghart said that when the name was spelled Buckhart it could only be a mistake as the true name was Burghart, although he was often called Buckhart.

Thomas McGeorge was born January 1758 in Hanover Co., Va., moved to Knox County and while living in Warren Co., Tenn., was allowed pension in 1833. His daughter Caroline married Israel Nance. Thomas McGeorge enlisted in Boutetourt Co., Va.

James McGeorge, born in Botetourte County, was a Revolutionary soldier who moved to Knox County. He married Anna la Force in 1795 and later settled on Strait Creek.

Henry Shackleford, born in King William County, Virginia, 1748 and christened at the Manken-Hick Church as soon as he was 16. He came to Harlan County about 1800. He said he served a tour as substitute for his brother John Shakleford. Apparently Shakleford was the correct spelling.

Berry Cawood, Revolutionary soldier, enlisted at the age of 17 in Washington Co., Va. Most of his work was Indian scouting and spying. In 1778 he went to Illinois with Col. George Rogers Clark, where they captured some British troops and marched them back to Fort Harrod, where he received his discharge. He later got married and when married only three weeks was drafted. He died in Harlan County 1848 at Cawood. Three of his children were named Berry, John and Joseph.

Ephriam Orsborne (Osburn, Ausborne), Pension R 7822 Va. He was 80 years old when he applied for pension, said he served under Capt. Enoch Osburn. He lived to be 100 years old and died in 1852 in Harlan County. Samuel Hord (Horde, Hoard, Howard), born in Buckingham Co., Va., 1762, died in Harlan County, 1840. He enlisted in 1778 and was at Yorktown when Cornwallis surrendered. He came into Harlan County about 1792, and settled at Mount Pleasant.

Henry Smith, Revolutionary soldier, Pension 30686, born in Brunswick Co., Va., about 1762, married Elizabeth Ledford in South Carolina, 1792. They came to Poor Fork, Harlan County, and had a large family: Sally married John Creech; Naomi (Omey); Robert Smith married Polly Smith, 1830; John Dixon officiated. Stacy Smith married William Turner 1824, John Lewis officiated. Polly Smith wife of John E. Smith; William Smith; Henry Smith; John H. Smith married Hannah Branson 1835, daughter of Henry Branson. She died in 1859. Hannah Smith married Capt. John Bailey in

1820, son of "Thumbie" John. She died and he married again.

Jonathan Smith married Cristeal (Christian) Jenkins, daughter of William Jenkins, in 1830. She died 1854 at age 30.

Stephen Jones, Revolutionary soldier, born Aug. 19, 1750, in St. Mary's County, Md., entered service in 1779. He died on Jones Creek where he is buried, and was drawing a pension at the time of his death. He mentioned son Zachariah, in his pension application when he was 83 years old in 1834. Known children were: Johnny, Hiram, Gabriel, Lucy, Sally, Zachariah, Elijah, Stephen.

The French and Indian War followed the Revolutionary War and the last battle was considered to have taken place in Indiana, near Lafayette, at a place called Prophet Town. Colonel Elijay Green of Tan Yard Hill served in this war. He was the son of Lewis and Esther (Easter) Kilgore Green. He was born in Virginia in 1786 and died in Kentucky in 1854. He married Sarah Hendricks (Hendrix).

During the War of 1812 the British burned the Capitol in Washington.

Andrew Bailey, born July 6, 1792, joined the Kentucky Militia in 1813. He was sent to Canada where he was in the battle when Dunlap was defeated. On April 18, 1814, he married Anna Kelly who was born Jan. 7, 1796, in Lee County, Va., and the soldier died in Harlan County in 1851.

Col. George Brittain, known as "General" Brittain, served from 1812-1814. He owned a large estate on Brittain's Branch of Martin's Fork known as Brittain's Hill. It is said that he attended the first Kentucky Constitution held at Danville when that was the capital of Kentucky.

Col. William Green, son of Lewis and Esther Kilgore Green, served in the War of 1812, born 1791 and died 1869, and is buried on Tan Yard Hill.

Captain Ninium Hoskins was in the War of 1812 and was living on Pucketts Creek at that time.

Stephen Rice, uncle of Ben A. Rice from Tazewell, Tenn., served in the War of 1812. He married Rebecca Woolum at the home of James Woolum and Rosannah Henderson and Mary R. Culton testified that they had known them since childhood. He received land grant in 1850, applied for pension in 1871 and was drawing a pension at the time of his death, Feb. 15, 1887.

Elias Smith served as a Colonel in the War of 1812. He was the grandfather of Emily Smith who married Samuel Clay Howard in 1876.

Capt. Benjamin Harris received Bounty Land for his service in the War of 1812. His first wife was Elizabeth Weaver and his second wife was Sarah S. Buckhart. He died at the age of 83, April 1861, and his widow applied for pension, when she was 47 years of age. He was born in 1778 in Virginia, the son of John Harris, and died in Harlan County. His widow described him as being about 5 feet 10 inches tall, fair complexion and light hair. He married Sara S. Buckhart January 16, 1854, by William Bailey, a minister. Her sister Nancy E. Ledford stated that her sister Sarah Buckhart Harris died in 1901 and left no heirs.

The War with Mexico occurred under President James Knox Polk. General Zachary Taylor was the hero of that war.

Here in Harlan County on March 4, 1849, the day that General Taylor was sworn in at the inauguration, Samuel Clay Howard was born. His parents told him that it was a cold raw day and the stock and cattle could hardly face the weather. The chickens huddled near the barn and his father fed the chickens hot meal-mush laced with red pepper to warn them.

Colonel Jonathan P. Smith entered the war in 1846 and married Flora Ann Metcalf in 1848. His cousin Jonathan Smith married Mary Metcalf in 1850.

Captain David Green joined the war against Mexico in 1846. He was born on Tanyard Hill in 1808 and died on Browney's Creek.

As of September 23, 1962, the *Harlan Daily Enterprise* published the following article:

"On a day early in May, 1912, 'came Leander Russel and

filed his application for pension' as a veteran of the Civil War, read Harlan County court record books of that time.

"Russell was not the only confederate veteran in the county at that time. Also filing for the pension were: Samuel P. Stewart, Calvin Unthank, Jonathan A. Bailey, George W. Blackburn, William Lankford, John R. Blevins and Carr Eldridge. Women, apparently veterans' widows, filing for pension were: Marian K. Lankford, Sally Middleton, Margaret Blevins and Nancy Cloud.

"The applications for pension were made under 'the Act allowing pensions to Confederate Soldiers, which act was approved by the Governor and became a law at the signing of said Act in 1912.'

" 'Whoopee, here I come,' yelled James 'Red Fox' Farmer, as he topped the hill at Main Street many years ago. He was hired to run down to Pineville early one morning by John 'Grandad' Jones and John B. Turner to get a newspaper so they could read the news about the Civil War."

Although there was divided sympathy for the North and the South here in Harlan County, the list of Confederate soldiers from this County is incomplete:

William Brittain who married Lucy Ball was captured and died in a Yankee prison camp. He left his widow Lucy Ball Brittain and several children.

Gipson Ball, Catron's Creek, was captured at Cumberland Gap and taken to Camp Chase, Ohio, where he was kept prisoner until the war was over. He married Nicy Hensley, born No. Carolina.

Calve Unthank donned the grey during this war. He was the son of Ewell V. and Sarah Jones Unthank. She was the daughter of John Jones, the merchant.

Telitha and Lewis Green, Tan Yard Hill, had four sons who were in the Rebel army: Elias, William, Wilkerson and Robert; Robert Green was killed.

On the Union side the list is much longer: Jacob Batner or Botner donned the blue. He was born 1834 and died 1911. He had four brothers who served but I do not have their names.

WARS

James Brock was on the Union side in the Battle of Cumberland Gap and was was one of the retreating soldiers who hid in a cave to avoid being captured.

William Griffith, an officer in the Union Army, was killed at the battle of Vicksburg. His daughter, Ruth Jane Griffith, married James Brock, the Union soldier.

Gilbert Creech, brother of Enoch I, who were the sons of old John Creech and Sally Smith Creech (daughter of Henry Smith, the Revolutionary soldier), was caught by the Rebels, court-martialed, tried as a spy and hanged at Big Leather. The Rebels had a stockade somewhere northeast of Harlan County. Then Gilbert Creech's nephew's son William Creech joined the Union army at an early age. He married Sally Dixon of Poor Fork in 1866. Lieut. John G. Creech served in this war, the son of Enoch Creech I. The Creeches were often called Critch or Scritch.

George Shoop entered the Civil War on the Union side, was sent to Camp Douglass, Illinois, where he died and is buried near Chicago. His daughter, Hannah Shoop, married Enoch Creech II, brother to William, Henry and Joseph, son of Joseph Creech.

Randolph Browning, a Baptist preacher, drew a pension for services during the Civil War. He married Rebecca Howard in 1870.

Henry Skidmore was in the Union Army. The place known as Skidmore's Farm was owned by Henry Skidmore. He married Elizabeth Ledford in 1839 with P. Spurlock officiating.

John Cawood, descendant of Revolutionary soldier, Berry Cawood, joined the Union Army. He married Louisana Jones in 1835 with the officiating minister, E. Batner.

John Bull of Pucketts Creek was killed in the Civil War. He was the son of Britt Bull. Later the Bull family changed their name to Buell.

B. F. Gilbert was a Union soldier who died at Shields on Clover Fork at the age of 90 years. He married Mary Wynn November 3, 1869; witnesses: William Turner, William Gilbert and Sam R. Gilbert. He left the following children:

Henry G., J. M., Shields; W. M. Gilbert and Samuel, Va.; Miss Mince Gilbert, Le Junior; John C. Gilbert; Mrs. Bettie Cooper, Va., Mrs. Luddie Ball, Evarts; B. H. Gilbert; Mrs. Sudie Wormsley, Evarts; Jess Gilbert, Le Junior; Mrs. Emily Phillips, Va.; Mrs. Cecile Barnette and Mrs. Rosalee Creech, Le Junior.

Silas Woodson Kelly who fought on the Union side died at the age of 92 years at Dartmont. He left two sons, S. C. Kelly and A. Z. Kelly; two daughters, Mrs. M. J. Ball and Mrs. Sarah Fields. He married Rebecca Smith in 1858. He was born 1840 and died 1932.

Judge W. C. L. Huff served in the Union Army in Company E, 49th Infantry and was stationed at Camp Nelson. He was born in 1846 and joined the army when he was 17 and died at the age of 83 in 1929. He first married Susan Howard, a granddaughter of "Uncle" Wix Howard and his second wife was Elizabeth Farley. His brother Eli Huff lived on Catron's Creek and another brother Abner Huff lived on Poor Fork. He left three sons, H. H. Huff, I. A. Huff and J. M. Huff.

Henderson Howard, son of "Uncle" Wix, married Cameliza Leford in 1859, Nobel Smith officiated. He served in the Union Army.

James G. Howard, who married Matilda Howard, was killed while serving with the Union forces. He left two sons, Moses Wilkerson Howard and Elhanan Murphy Howard. He had named his first son after a famous soldier and after Moses Wilkerson Howard had sons, he named a son Elhanan Murphy Howard whom we know as "Dr. Murph," and he named his son Elhanan Murphy Howard, namesakes of the general.

John W. Forrester, born in 1838, was Lieutenant of his company on the Union side. He served in the 49th Volunteer Infantry in 1863. He was the son of Jeremiah Forrester who married Mary Osborne. John W. Forrester married Nancy Howard, daughter of John C. and Miltilda Brock Howard. He died at an early age in 1873 after a few years of married life. He left his widow and five children, J. Grant, James S.,

Mary J. who died young and Matilda Forrester, wife of Johnas Helton.

Francis Hall, Jr., entered Civil War on the Union side. He was proud of his nickname of "Hawse Rogue" because his job was to get horses for the Union soldiers. He was quite a character and during political meetings in town he would wave the flag and shout, "Live or die, sink or swim, I'm for the log cabin party." He married Easter Cawood, daughter of Joel Cawood.

His brother, James Hall of Poor Fork, was on the Union side. Their father, Francis Hall, Sr., was a brother to Alford Hall, a preacher and justice of the peace. His son Bill was called Bill-Alf Hall and is the father of Lily Hall Middleton, widow of Charles C. Middleton.

Cam Hurst was on the Union side. He married Mary "Pop" Rice, daughter of Zelpha and Ben Ajax Rice.

Henry Lewis Howard, father of Hobart and Orville Howard, was on the Union side, later became Commonwealth Attorney.

Adron Nolen was in the Union Army and he was killed near his home on Pine Mountain. It is said that he was shot by Rebel spies. He was the son of "Uncle" John Noland.

C. F. C. Nolan joined the Union Army. His grandfather was John Noland from North Carolina. His great-grandfather was John Turner, a Revolutionary soldier. C. F. C. Nolan was born 1845 and died 1923. His will in Book II names

 Mary Jane Nolan Skidmore (wife of Jeems)
 J. M. Nolan who married Nancy W. Smith, father of Chad J. Nolan
 Dr. William Turner Nolan who married Prescious Cornett
 B. F. Nolan
 dau. Nancy Nolan Howard, dau. Betty Nolan Marshall
 dau. Maggie L. Davisworth
 Dr. Joe W. Nolan who married Bertha Whithead
 Gillis B. Nolen

and Stephen Nolan (son of John H. Nolen who died 1921)

John Robert Rice, son of Ben A. and Zelpha Rice, joined the Union side. He was a brother of Henry Clay Rice and his second wife was a sister to Henry Rice's wife. They were Serepta Eager and Sarah Mandy Eager whose folks were Rebels.

Thomas Skelton Ward joined the Union Drum Corps when he was a lad. He had four brothers on the Union side from Strait Creek, Isaac, John, Alex and Frank Ward. T. S. Ward married Mary Francis Jones, daughter of Maston Green Jones and Sarah Lane Jones. He died at the age of 92 years and was affectionately called "Grandaddy." His wife

Thomas Skelton Ward—Civil War Veteran. The girls are two of his wife's great-nieces—Roxie and Lizzie Bailey—and Mae Van Gorder, one of the first stenographers in Harlan.

died during a meningitis epidemic and he never remarried. He lived with his maiden daughter Nannie. His other children were John Ancil Ward; Thomas S.; William; Mastin Green; and Ollie who married Will Eager.

John M. Pittman was born in Harlan County (now Bell) Nov. 22, 1843, and enlisted during the Civil War. He married Malinda Hoskins, December 11, 1867, and became a Baptist minister and preached until he was unable to do so. He died at East Bernstadt in 1930 when he was 87 years old.

Harlan County like all of Kentucky was divided as to sympathy. It is said that most of the residents on Poor Fork and Pine Mountain and Strait Creek and some of the Cumberland River folks were on the side of the Union while residents of Clover Fork, Martin's Fork, Catron's Creek, the lower end of Cumberland River, Cumberland Ford, Clear Creek and Yellow Creek were southern sympathizers. Some of the residents called it the "War of the Rebellion" and people in sympathy with the Confederate side were called "Rebels." There is a large overhanging rock cliff about four miles north of the county seat, in sight of the present

REBEL ROCK
Pine Mountain, U.S. 421, near the Mountain Aire Motel

Lewallen Court Motel, which was called "Rebel Rock." This rock was used by Rebel scouts to hide under the reconnoiter which would furnish a quick hiding place for the scouts if they encountered unfriendly groups.

Harlan County suffered not only from both armies who commandeered everything in sight, but from bands of renegade pseudo soldiers, men who had stolen uniforms off dead men and went over the county stealing from the settlers. The Harlan County courthouse was burned because of this kind of raid. A group of men burned the courthouse in the adjoining Virginia county of Lee and in retaliation the Harlan courthouse was burned by Rebels who blamed Union sympathizers for burning the Lee County courthouse.

Every horse, mule, cow, pig, cured meat, farm products, blankets and even cured drinking gourds and vessels were taken from the settlers. George Washington Eager, who lived on Catron's Creek, was born in 1803 and at the time of the Civil War was not a young man. There were no banks close by, so everyone was suspected of hiding or burying silver. During the war a group of villians masquerading as soldiers came to the Eager home one day before daylight and threatened to kill him if he did not show them where his money was hidden. They took him outside to a peach tree and lifted him off the ground trying to make him tell if he had any money. His wife, Sally Clark Eager, had a purse with about four dollars in silver, hidden in her clothing and for fear they might search her, she poked the purse through a hole in the log chinking and saved their little silver hoard. The robbers took their pots, pans, coverlids, featherbeds and everything they could load on pack mules. Later a posse was formed which was joined by two of the Eager girls. Following the trail, they found the goods hidden in a cache on Pine Mountain and recovered the goods.

It was during the Civil War that President Lincoln's administration levied taxes on incomes, estates, etc., on account of the rising cost of financing the war. The first Income Tax Law was made in July, 1862.

Kentucky remained loyal and yet a Confederate unit of

WARS

government was established, so many of the Kentuckians volunteered in different armies, and the government had a draft program. Kentucky had a star in the Confederate Flag and also retained its star in the Federal Flag.

Other troubles beset the people and during the Civil War there was an outbreak of smallpox. A home which had been commandeered for a hospital for wounded soldiers, located at the Narrows on a high bank overlooking Cumberland River near the Ford, was almost washed away by the biggest flood known to old-timers. The water rose so high that the wounded had to be carried into the loft until the water had receded.

Sand Cave and Gunpowder Cave were both used by soldiers on both sides. They are located near Cumberland Gap and Stone Mountain. When the Rebels were retreating they used these caves and when the Yanks were in need of a hiding place, they used them. My uncle, William T. Rice, once found a belt buckle with "C.S.A." in Sand Cave and one wonders if a wounded soldier crept in there to die and that was all that remained. It is said that these caves were used by the Indians during their raids to hide their looted treasures.

In 1934 the Gray Clad Vets held a reunion which was attended by 1,600 old soldiers, most of them in their middle eighties. I believe this reunion was held in Tennessee.

A true story of the Civil War was handed down to Suddie Brittain Ward (Mrs. John Ancil Ward) by her mother who was a widow during the Civil War before Mrs. Ward was born, and before she was remarried.

A young man named James Renfro married Susan Burch and they settled at Wasioto on a large farm where they raised everything they ate and wore, except salt, coffee, queensware and such items as calico, muslins and silks. Their furniture and equipment was made from trees on the place and they had four daughters: Anne, Jennie, Lucy and Ruth Renfro. James Renfro died and left this young widow with her four daughters who continued to run the farm with the help of some darkies who lived on the place. She and the colored folks did all the work, raising crops, sheep, pigs, chickens, cane for sorghum, corn and other staples. They had planted an orchard and had a "stand" of beegums which produced their honey and they tapped the maple for their syrup and sugar.

They had heard rumors of the Civil War but it had not really touched them and they continued to live as usual until late one cold fall day, a neighbor came running by to warn them that the soldiers encamped at Cumberland Gap were going through the country foraging and commandeering everything for their encampment. The Renfro household was in order for the winter: they had finished putting away corn, sweet potatoes, apples, sorghum and had slaughtered their first pork of the season, had made sausage and rendered lard. Their neighbor advised them to bury everything they possibly could so they began to dig a long trench across the yard and lined it with hay and placed all their provisions in this trench, except what they would need for the next few days. They covered the trench with dirt and raked the fresh dirt over smoothly, moved equipment and implements around so that the trench could not be detected. Then she had the darky Zeke take their mule and horse over behind the orchard in a swag to tether it near the forest where it was partly hidden from view. The horse was really a pet mare named Maud and though she was used to work, plough, and go to Mill, the whole family loved Maud.

It was getting daylight by the time they were through with their farm chores and they were cooking a breakfast of sausage, corncakes, sorghum, butter and milk when they heard hoofbeats and looking out they saw the soldiers riding up to the house, so the Widow Renfro met them at the door and invited them in for breakfast. While they were eating she explained that she was a widow and had very little to offer and she hoped they would pass by without raiding her place. After breakfast the soldiers were mounting their horses to leave without taking anything, when the pet mare poked her head around the corner of the house and the soldiers took her away despite the pleading of the widow and her small daughters. Now the whole place was in consternation over the loss of their pet mare and they felt very sad. Late that afternoon Mrs. Renfro told her overseer, Zeke, to have the mule ready to ride to Cumberland Gap the next morning at daybreak and both she and Zeke would go and try to get the mare. It was a distance of about 16 miles from her home to the Gap, over little Log Mountain, Big Log Mountain and Yellow Creek Break. Parts of the road were too rough to ride over so they walked part way and took turns riding part way. When they got to the Gap, they could see signs of activity and smell food cooking. She sent Zeke in to request an audience with the officer in charge and he politely invited her in. They were having their noon dinner and the officer ordered a plate for her and Zeke. She said the food tasted good because they were right hungry from their long trip. The meal consisted of ham, sweet potatoes, cabbage, cornbread and coffee. Coffee had been scarce so they particularly enjoyed the coffee. Mrs. Renfro told the officer that she was a widow with four little girls and that they could not get along without their mare. The officer told her that if she could identify her horse that she could take it back with her. They went to the corral where many horses were enclosed and Zeke had already found the mare they called Maud. When the mare saw her mistress, Maud held up her head and whinnied loud and clear. "Whee-ee-ee, Whee-hee-ee, Whee-ee-ee." The officer in charge said, "Madam, the horse is yours."

Susan Burch Renfro later married Carlo Brittain and their daughter Sudie did not know the name or rank of the officer who was so gallant and kind to her mother. A son, Carlo Brittain, Jr., became an admiral in the United States Navy. He married Mary Baldwin, from Richmond, Ky., and they had one son who is a Naval officer. Sudie Brittain Ward married John Ancil Ward II and his father Thomas Skelton Ward along with four brothers served on the Union side. The Renfros were southern sympathizers, as were the Brittains.

Luise Bethune Duffield, widow of General W. W. Duffield, came to Harlan County with her son Will Ward Duffield and daughter Louise Duffield in 1904. Her husband was a general on the Union side, and they used to tell a story about General Duffield being wounded during the Civil War. He was recuperating at a southern home where some of the wounded had been quartered and his wife went to this home to nurse him during his convalescence. After they returned to their home the Duffields thought it would be nice to send the family a present in appreciation of the use of their home so they sent a silver tea service. They said that when word got around that General Duffield had sent a gift to people on the Confederate side that there was talk of a court-martial. Anyway General Duffield and his wife Luise are buried at Arlington Cemetery.

Mrs. Duffield was of French extraction and when they were married, her husband took her to his home which was on Woodward Lane, a few miles from Detroit, and I understand that this is now a busy street.

Luise Bethune Duffield, widow of General Will Ward Duffield—Union Army.

Their son Will Ward Duffield organized the first Boy Scout Troop in Harlan and the Allegheny region in 1912. His great-uncle, Reverend George Duffield, Jr., 1818-1888, a Presbyterian minister, wrote the words to the hymn "Stand Up for Jesus." Rev. George Duffield, Sr., was a chaplain in the Revolutionary Army.

When Will Ward Duffield organized the Harlan Boy Scout Troop No. 1, there were about 58 boys on the rolls, among whom were: Earl Brock, Virgil Brock, Taylor Forester, John W. Forester, J. Arna Gregory, Carlo B. Gross, Hampton H. Huff, Raymond Jenkins, Owen Kelly, Fred C. Lewis, Orville Howard, Herbert C. Smith, Joe Cawood, George R. Pope, J. R. Rice, Clyde Rice, Ralph E. Smith, Hobart S. Walker, and many others. The leader of the troop under Mr. Duffield was Tom S. Ward, Jr. When Mr. Duffield was appointed Deputy Scout Commissioner, he was one of the first in America. The members of this troop paid for their own uniforms.

Although he was the son of a Yankee General, Will Ward Duffield was a member of the Democratic party and was at one time Mayor of Harlan. He came to Harlan County as an engineer and geologist in charge of Kentenia Corporation, a large landholding company, the largest stockholders being a family named Davis from South Yarmouth, Mass., and the Delano family who owned vast acreage in Kentucky, Tennessee and Virginia. Will Ward Duffield is buried in Rest Haven Cemetery, Harlan County, and his grave monument was bought by Boy Scouts and friends. He served in many offices of the Harlan Presbyterian Church and was a member of the Centre College Board at the time of his death in 1939. He was born in 1859.

When the United States became involved in war with Spain, there were about seventy-five from this county who volunteered. Here is an incomplete list of the Harlan boys:

Ulysses Botner, Carlo Cawood, Bob Hall, Billie G. Farler, Enos M. Johnson, Jim Kelly, Chad J. Nolan, Lt. John H. Nolan, Jeff Rice, Will Roark, George Smith, Melvin Gregory. George Smith was sent to the Philippines and contracted smallpox, he died and is buried over there. He was the son of David Hill and Susan Turner Smith,

A company was organized from this district, known as Company H, of the 4th Kentucky Volunteer Regiment. Colonel Dave Colson and Lt. John Howard were from Middlesboro; Capt. Jim S. Forester, Lt. John Bradley Carter, George Creech, of Harlan; Dave Elders and his son Bill Elders, Evarts; Henry Hall, Burnam Sergeant, James Stewart and his two sons, Marion Stewart and Lee Stewart, Cawood; Oriah Witt, Clospint, Bruce Jones, Williamsburg; James Brittain, Catron's Creek; Will Harris, Clover Fork; Milt Hall, Grays Knob; Tom King, Evarts; Green Osborne, Turcle Creek; Dr. Frank Kelly, Walter Kelly, Evarts; Hiram Hensley, R. L. Howard (brother to Milty), Rich Blanton, Molus; Finley Lankford, Turcle Creek; Henry Pace and Jim Pace (twins), Yokum; Sgt. Dillard Saylor, Molus; Silas Middleton, Chas. C. Middleton, John Middleton, brothers; Jim K. Middleton and old Ben Middleton; Abner and Leander Skidmore, brothers; J. M. Unthank, Milt Unthank and Carter Unthank, Will Roark, and while living in Harlan, Zeb A. Stewart, attorney, applied for pension on account of services in the Spanish American War when he lived at Murray, Kentucky. He enlisted at age 22. He died at Frankfort January 1962, age 84. He was chairman of the Harlan County Draft Board in World War I.

Ulysses Botner enlisted in the Spanish-American War and served three years in the Philippines. He was a brother of Isaac and John Botner, son of Elias and Matilda Botner.

Lieut. John Bradley Carter is the son of Nannie Cawood and John Crockett Carter. He first married Amelia Howard, daughter of Samuel Clay and Emily Jane Smith Howard. He and his daughter Ruby live on Ivy Street. She was a Captain in the Wacs during World War II. Another daughter, Florence Clay, married Bryan Whitfield II. A son, Howard Carter, married "Peaches" Sampson. Another son, Warren Carter, is the son of his second marriage to Susan Warren.

WARS

JEFF RICE, Spanish-American War   JIM KELLY, Spanish-American War

These two first cousins left together to join the Army, 1898. They were in the Cavalry.

Capt. James S. Forester married Mary Smith, daughter of David Hill Smith and Susan Turner Smith.

R. L. Howard, brother of Squire J. B. Milty Howard, S. B. "Buck" Howard. Willis Howard and Mrs. Ed Garrett, served in this War.

Lt. John Howard and Colonel David Colson were from Middlesboro, Ky.

Enos M. Johnson was married 1880 to Jerusha Johnson, granddaughter of "Uncle Wix" Howard and daughter of Ephram Johnson.

Jim Kelly, son of Joe S. and Mary Rice-Hurst Kelly, married Addie Howard, daughter of Elhanan Murphy Howard.

Chad J. Nolan, son of James M. and Nancy Smith Nolan, married Mary "Mollie" L. Carter, daughter of John Crockett Carter and Nannie Cawood Carter.

Lt. John H. Nolen, son of C. F. C. Nolan, was in Company L, 4th Kentucky Infantry, and is buried at Nolansburg, Ky. He was born Oct. 4, 1871, and died March 13, 1921.

Jeff Rice, son of Henry Clay Rice and Sarah Mandy Eager Rice, married Minta Wilson, daughter of Lucy Ward and Elhanan Wilson.

Charles C. Middleton was in the Spanish-American War, the son of B. F. and Mary Jane Middleton. Two of his brothers, Silas and John, died in 1907. His other brothers were Mose, Marion, Berry and Sam Middleton, and his two sisters were Mrs. Addie King and Mrs. Maud Metcalf. When he died Sept. 26, 1943, he left his widow Lily Hall Middleton, daughter of Jim, known as Alf's Jim Hall, two sons, Merle and Edwin R., and a daughter Mrs. John Christian. John Middleton, brother to Charles and Silas, served in the 4th Kentucky Volunteers. Silas Middleton, brother to Charles and John, married Alice Smith, a descendant of the Revolutionary soldier, Henry Smith.

I do not know the relationship of "Old" Ben Middleton and Jim K. Middleton to the above.

George Creech, son of Enoch II and Hannah Shoop Creech, married Canna McIntyre.

Bob Hall, a bachelor now 84 years old, who was sent to Alabama and later to the Philippines where he contracted malaria, received disability. His parents were France Hall and Easter Cawood Hall; her father was Joel Cawood.

James M. Unthank was born Oct. 19, 1875, and married Martilla Howard. Carter Unthank is brother to J. M. Unthank.

Carlo Brittain Cawood, son of Hiram and Sally Brittain Cawood, descended from Berry Cawood, the Revolutionary soldier. He married Ora Cornett, daughter of Ella Amanda Hurst and Arthur Blankenship Cornett.

Hiram Hensley, brother of Sadie Hensley Day-Saylor, married Sallie Kelly, daughter of Joe S. and Mary (Pop) Rice Hurst-Kelly.

Dillard Saylor, brother to Radford Saylor, was Sergeant of Company H.

Melvin Gregory was a brother of Mrs. Zada Rutherford and Mrs. Maggie Hoskins.

www.ingramcontent.com/pod-product-compliance
Lightning Source LLC
Chambersburg PA
CBHW060521080526
44586CB00012B/571